T0334077

Cambridge Elements

Elements in New Religious Movements
edited by
Rebecca Moore
San Diego State University
Founding Editor
James R. Lewis
Wuhan University

THE UNIFICATION
CHURCH MOVEMENT

Michael L. Mickler
Unification Theological Seminary

CAMBRIDGE
UNIVERSITY PRESS

Shaftesbury Road, Cambridge CB2 8EA, United Kingdom

One Liberty Plaza, 20th Floor, New York, NY 10006, USA

477 Williamstown Road, Port Melbourne, VIC 3207, Australia

314–321, 3rd Floor, Plot 3, Splendor Forum, Jasola District Centre, New Delhi – 110025, India

103 Penang Road, #05–06/07, Visioncrest Commercial, Singapore 238467

Cambridge University Press is part of Cambridge University Press & Assessment, a department of the University of Cambridge.

We share the University's mission to contribute to society through the pursuit of education, learning and research at the highest international levels of excellence.

www.cambridge.org
Information on this title: www.cambridge.org/9781009241458

DOI: 10.1017/9781009241465

© Michael L. Mickler 2022

This publication is in copyright. Subject to statutory exception and to the provisions of relevant collective licensing agreements, no reproduction of any part may take place without the written permission of Cambridge University Press & Assessment.

First published 2022

A catalogue record for this publication is available from the British Library.

ISBN 978-1-009-24145-8 Paperback
ISSN 2635-232X (online)
ISSN 2635-2311 (print)

Cambridge University Press & Assessment has no responsibility for the persistence or accuracy of URLs for external or third-party internet websites referred to in this publication and does not guarantee that any content on such websites is, or will remain, accurate or appropriate.

The Unification Church Movement

Elements in New Religious Movements

DOI: 10.1017/9781009241465
First published online: November 2022

Michael L. Mickler
Unification Theological Seminary

Author for correspondence: Michael L. Mickler, mm@uts.edu

Abstract: This Element recounts the tumultuous history of the Unification Church Movement (UCM), deriving from the messianic ministry of Moon Sun Myung (1920–2012). It begins with the UCM's origins in Korea and traces its development into a global conglomerate of churches, related nonprofit organizations, and for-profit businesses. Known for its mass marriages, or "International Marriage Blessings," the UCM has been one of the most controversial new religious movements throughout the world, particularly in Japan and the West. The post-Moon UCM is a textbook case of a new religious movement transitioning from its founding to succeeding generations, a transition marked by this emergence of schismatic organizations. Utilizing both external documents and internal UCM sources, the account highlights the leading personalities, organizations, and circumstances which facilitated the UCM's rise, present challenges, and future development.

Keywords: Sun Myung Moon, Unification Church, Family Federation, True Parents, Divine Principle

© Michael L. Mickler 2022

ISBNs: 9781009241458 (PB), 9781009241465 (OC)
ISSNs: 2635-232X (online), 2635-2311 (print)

Contents

1 Introduction

The Unification Church/Movement (UCM) refers to an international constellation of churches, related nonprofit organizations, and for-profit businesses that derive from the messianic ministry of Moon Sun Myung (1920–2012). It was established in Korea as the Holy Spirit Association for the Unification of World Christianity (HSA-UWC) in 1954. Its founding vision was to unite Christian denominations, bring unity among the world's religions, and, on that basis, usher in the Kingdom of Heaven on earth. Followers understand Moon to be the Lord of the Second Advent, that is, Christ's second coming. He is believed to have received his commission from Jesus Christ in a series of encounters beginning in 1935. Moon and his wife, Han Hak Ja (b. 1943), are referred to as the "True Parents of Humankind." The UCM is known for its mass marriages, or "International Marriage Blessings," involving many thousands of participants at high-profile venues such as Seoul Olympic Stadium and Madison Square Garden. As the UCM's central sacrament, the Blessing is understood to be a process through which men and women come into union with each other, engraft to the True Parents, are reconciled with God, and thereby, according to the UCM, reconstitute themselves as a new humanity.

The core beliefs of the UCM are contained in *Wolli-Kangron* (1966), its primary doctrinal and religious text, translated from Korean into two official English edition texts, *Divine Principle* (1973) and *Exposition of the Divine Principle* (1996). Both texts employ familiar theological categories (creation, fall, Christology, resurrection, predestination, Trinity, providential history, eschatology) but interpret them in ways that highlight an overriding emphasis on the family. God, as parent, is the source of both masculinity and femininity, and the texts specifically identify the Holy Spirit as the feminine aspect of the Godhead. The texts similarly propound a family-based interpretation of sin, locating the human fall in adulterous and premature sexuality communicated symbolically in Genesis. Humankind's original ancestors became false parents who perpetuated a fallen lineage and fallen history. Salvation hinges on the restoration of True Parents. Jesus came as the second Adam with the mission to find a bride, or second Eve, with whom he would establish a true family, true lineage, and true history. The crucifixion was a tragic mistake which ushered in a secondary course led by the resurrected Christ and Holy Spirit (the second Eve) who, as spiritual True Parents, offer rebirth. Upon the foundation of Christianity, the third Adam will find a prepared bride (the third Eve), establish a new lineage, and consummate human history. The texts teach that humanity at present is in the Last Days, that Christ will come again, born in the flesh on earth, and that the nation from which Christ will come is Korea.[1]

---

[1] *Exposition of the Divine Principle* (New York: Holy Spirit Association for the Unification of World Christianity, 1996), vii, 9, 19, 54–61, 114–19, 171–72, 383, 385–93, 396–407.

Although founded as an association, HSA-UWC immediately took on the characteristics of a church and became known in Korea as *Tongil Kyohae,* or Unification Church (UC). The UC organized congregations, conducted regular worship services, published sacred texts, evangelized in Seoul and rural districts, developed distinctive ceremonies and rituals, collected tithes and offerings, and, during the 1950s, dispatched missionaries to England (1954), Japan (1958), and the United States (1959). The UC sent missionaries to continental Europe during the 1960s and worldwide in 1975, establishing churches or a presence in some 185 nations by the turn of the twenty-first century. During this period, the UC took on the profile of a social movement, i.e., the UCM. In 1963, Moon organized the Tongil Group, a for-profit South Korean business conglomerate or *chaebol,* associated with the UC. Its purpose was to provide revenue for the church and church-related projects. The Tongil Group disbursed funds through the Tongil Foundation, which supported HSA-UWC as well as its initiatives in education, culture, and the arts, the media, and public advocacy. The UC exported this model, in different forms, to Japan, the United States, and mission countries.

In the mid-1990s, Moon set up the Family Federation for World Peace and Unification (FFWPU or Family Federation) as a successor organization to the UC. Partly due to the downfall of communism, which the UCM regarded as the chief obstacle to the establishment of God's sovereignty on earth, Moon publicly declared in 1992 that he and Hak Ja Han Moon were "the True Parents of humanity ... the Savior, the Lord of the Second Advent, the Messiah."[2] In 1993, he proclaimed the beginning of the Completed Testament Age. An oral tradition, consisting of Moon's sermons and speeches, previously viewed as a supplement to *Divine Principle,* began to displace or at least compete with the official texts. Moon encouraged this development and in 1998 announced that his words, collected in several volumes, were to be the authoritative Completed Testament Age canon. In 2004, the Family Federation published a new set of Moon's words titled *Cheon Seong Gyeong* or "Heavenly Scripture," nearly 2,500 pages collected from some 500 volumes of his speeches. Prior to his death in 2012, Moon assembled his "last words to humankind" in the form of "Eight Great Textbooks" which included his collected sermons, *Exposition of Divine Principle,* and other works. After Moon's death, Hak Ja Han Moon, his widow, oversaw publication of a new set of Holy Scriptures, *Cheon Seong Gyeong* (revised), *Pyeong Hwa Gyeong* (peace messages), and *Cham Bumo Gyeong* (True Parents' life course), which included her words and historical role.

---

[2] S. M. Moon, "Becoming Leaders and Building a World of Peace," *Today's World* 13, no. 9 (October–November, 1992): 4.

Moon intended the Family Federation to be a religious but nonsectarian organization that extended "the sacramental Unificationist marriage blessing to non-Unificationist couples" and concentrated on "peace initiatives."[3] He envisioned a world in which religious barriers would be overcome and regularly introduced utopian projects ranging from an international peace highway to the establishment of a religious assembly within the structure of the United Nations. At the same time, Moon was a pragmatic institution-builder. He did not allow visionary endeavors to compromise the religious tradition and network of institutions he had constructed over more than four decades of effort. Therefore, despite proclaiming an era of families, he took steps to ensure that the Family Federation remained a hierarchically based organization subject to his direction. In addition, because the UC was legally incorporated in multiple countries, the Family Federation and UC continued to coexist. In reality, the two organizations were indistinguishable and interchangeable. Nevertheless, Family Federation was the preferred designation after 1994.

Moon fit Weber's classic description of the charismatic leader as one "endowed with supernatural, superhuman, or at least exceptional powers and qualities."[4] This was an organizational strength, but also a liability, as he provided a focus for UCM detractors. His Asian origins, presumed connections to the Korean government, apparent extreme wealth, alleged sexual improprieties, and even his name, afforded grist to enemies who derided followers as "Moonies" and the UCM as a cult. In the United States, efforts to deny the UCM tax-exempt status, prevent its foreign missionaries from entering the country, and forcefully extract members from the movement through kidnapping and deprogramming put the UCM on the defensive, causing it to spend millions in litigation, sparking government investigations, and generating widespread public hostility. A 1977 Gallup poll found that Sun Myung Moon "elicited one of the most negative responses ever reported by a major poll," exceeded only by "Nikita Khrushchev and Fidel Castro."[5] Moon was subsequently convicted on tax evasion charges and served thirteen months at Danbury Federal Correctional Institute, Connecticut (1984–5), actions supporters contended were driven by religious animus and selective prosecution.[6] During the same period, the Unification Church USA gained legal recognition as a bona fide religion with tax-exemption privileges, public solicitation rights, access to missionary visas,

---

[3] Bromley, D. and A. Blonner, "From the Unification Church to the Unification Movement and Back," *Nova Religio* 16, no. 2 (2012): 88–89.

[4] M. Weber, *The Theory of Social and Economic Organization* (New York: Free Press, 1964), 398.

[5] Gallup, G. and D. Poling, *The Search for America's Faith* (Nashville, TN: Abingdon, 1980), 28–29.

[6] C. Sherwood, *Inquisition: The Prosecution and Persecution of Rev. Moon* (Washington, DC: Regnery Publishing, 1991).

and protection for members against deprogramming.[7] Scholars also deconstructed the brainwashing theory of member affiliation.[8]

This Element is neither a sociological nor a theological analysis but a historical account of the UCM's origins and development. As such, it makes use of sources not previously utilized, some of which are not published. The bulk of these are UCM materials: periodicals, books, memoirs, speeches, and the like that document the UCM's tumultuous history. The account is intended to be as comprehensive as possible in highlighting the leading personalities, organizations, and circumstances that facilitated the UCM's emergence, but it does not include numerous regional and localized initiatives, many in the developing world, which did not factor into the UCM's core trajectories. Rather, the narrative focuses on the UCM's mainstream development centered primarily on Sun Myung Moon and his family.

The Element divides UCM history into four chronological sections. First is the UCM's prehistory. Section 2, "Beginnings," covers Moon's background and early life (1920–45) and his pre-UCM early ministry (1945–54). The section examines his family background, major formative influences in his early life, his Christ experience (1935), and decade-long preparation for ministry (1935–45). It also details his initial efforts to gain followings in Seoul (1945–6) and Pyongyang (1946–8), his imprisonment in a North Korean labor camp (1948–50), and his effort to restart his ministry in the South (1951–3). There are similarities between the UCM and other Korean new religious movements and messianic variants. However, Moon's interest in the sciences; education; economics; media, culture, and the arts; and politics went well beyond most of these groups. The UCM's growth into a global movement is rooted in Sun Myung Moon's biography.

Moon and four followers founded the HSA-UWC or Unification Church in 1954. Section 3 follows the church amid much opposition as it became solidified in South Korea during the 1950s. Moon's 1960 marriage to Hak Ja Han marked a transition, as HSA-UWC became a more broadly based movement during the 1960s, incorporating economic, cultural, and educational components. Prior to that, the UC had sent missionaries to Japan (1958) and the United States (1959). Despite Korea's history of enmity with Japan, HSA-UWC Japan was a success story. It outstripped Korea's membership and became the resource engine that fueled the UCM's global advance while sparking intense domestic opposition. Moon viewed the United States as the gateway to the world and

---

[7] M. Mickler, "No Stranger to Litigation: Court Cases Involving the Unification Church/Family Federation in the United States," in *Reactions to the Law by Minority Religions*, eds. E. Barker and J. Richardson (London: Routledge, 2021), 80.

[8] E. Barker, *The Making of a Moonie: Choice or Brainwashing?* (Oxford: Blackwell Publishing, 1984).

shifted the focus of his ministry there during the 1970s. In 1975, the UCM sent missionary teams to ninety-five nations. During the 1980s, the UCM further diversified and expanded its ability to exert influence, notably through *The Washington Times*, established in 1982.

During the 1990s, the UCM entered a new phase characterized by more open public acknowledgments of its messianic premises. Section 4 highlights HSA-UWC's transition to the Family Federation for World Peace and Unification (FFWPU), the messianic trajectories that followed, and the final years of Sun Myung Moon's ministry, which included a consummate though largely symbolic effort to construct a Unification-styled nation, referred to as *Cheon Il Guk* ("the nation of cosmic peace and harmony"). In addition to lingering negative stereotypes, Moon's last years were marked by internal fissures, mainly among his adult children who had assumed leadership roles. His death in 2012 accentuated these. However, Hak Ja Han Moon, his widow, acted decisively to consolidate her position as FFWPU's head. She pulled FFWPU past the crisis of Moon's death, withstood internal criticism, and developed a distinct global ministry. The long-term future of the FFWPU was still uncertain, but Hak Ja Han proved herself a creative and resourceful leader in the mold of her late husband.

The UCM spawned minor schismatic groups during Moon's ministry, but this situation changed following his death. Two of his sons introduced a new dynamic, each claiming to be their father's rightful successor. Both definitively broke from the Family Federation, sought to discredit and displace their mother as leader of the UCM, opposed each other, and siphoned off FFWPU resources. Section 5 surveys early UCM splinter groups as well as the more formidable Moon family breakaway organizations. Early UCM splinter groups were an irritant but not a threat. Schismatic organizations led by the sons were a more serious problem. One refused to give up major UCM assets he controlled in Korea and the United States. The other began a gun-centered "Rod of Iron" ministry, refused to discontinue use of the trademarked HSA-UWC symbol, and went to court to have himself declared FFWPU leader. However, their conflict with FFWPU was asymmetrical: Organizations led by the brothers possessed a small percentage of FFWPU's membership.

The concluding section considers the UCM's future. It advances the thesis, put forward in an early study, that the UCM's origins "are genuinely humble, religious, and spiritual (which many doubt)" and that "the adaptability and solidarity" of the UCM is such that "we are dealing with a movement that is here to stay."[9] The conclusion acknowledges that this depiction of the UCM's

---

[9] F. Sontag, *Sun Myung Moon and the Unification Church* (Nashville, TN: Abingdon, 1977), 12.

origins is disputed by opponents and that it has not been able to entirely shed descriptions of it as a political organization, a business masquerading as a religion, or that it originated as a 1950s sex cult. It also acknowledges that the UCM faces formidable pressures to settle down into a form unrecognizable to its founders, or to split apart. In this respect, conclusions as to the UCM's future are provisional. Whether it seeks a denominational niche within which to perpetuate, whether it maintains its world-transforming fervor, or whether it does both will be key questions during the next stage of its development.

2 Beginnings

Since the late nineteenth century, some 500 new religions have established themselves in Korea.[10] They are diverse, deriving from shamanistic, Buddhist, neo-Confucian, and Christian traditions. However, many exhibit common traits including "a strong spirit of nationalism," expectation of a messianic figure to redeem people from suffering, "plans for a physical utopia and transformation of the present world into an ideal one," teachings divinely revealed to a founder, and syncretism, i.e., "efforts to integrate traditional patterns with the plethora of foreign influences."[11] While sharing these features, the UCM is unique among Korean new religions in its global reach. As noted, this development is rooted in the biography of Sun Myung Moon.

Moon's Background and Early Life

Yong Myung Moon (later Sun Myung Moon), was born on the sixth day of the first lunar month in 1920 (February 25) at 2221 Sang-sa Ri (village), Deok-eon District, Jeong-ju Township, Pyong-an Province, some 80 miles (almost 130 km) northwest of Pyongyang, in what is now North Korea. He was the second son of thirteen children, eight of whom survived, born to MOON Kyung-yoo (1893–1954) and KIM Kyung-gye (1888–1968). His paternal great-grandfather, Jong-ul, known as Sun-ok (1841–1918), settled in Sang-sa Ri where the majority of the thirty or so households were of the Nampyeong Moon clan. The extended family was prosperous, producing thousands of bushels of rice and providing hospitality to Koreans fleeing to Manchuria after their homes or land were confiscated by the Japanese. However, they fell on hard times after Moon's great uncle, Yun-guk (1877–1959), convinced them

---

[10] Yongbok, Y. and M. Introvigne, "Problems in Researching Korean New Religions: A Case Study of Daesoon Jinrihoe," *Journal of CESNUR* 2, no. 5 (September–October 2018): 84.

[11] J. S. Judah. "Introduction to the History and Beliefs of the Unification Church," in M. Mickler, *The Unification Church in America: A Bibliography and Research Guide* (New York: Garland, 1987), 4.

to sell family land under the guise of borrowing the money to invest in a coal mine. He then donated the funds to the Korean Provisional Government in Shanghai. Moon's immediate family was able to retain "three plots, about six acres, near the main house."[12]

Sources in English covering Moon's early life are meager. They are mainly limited to Moon's later, voluminous speeches which provided material for his autobiography, *As a Peace-Loving Global Citizen* (2009) and Michael Breen's *Sun Myung Moon: The Early Years, 1920–53* (1997), based on interviews with Moon's relatives and contemporaries. Although limited, they provide relevant biographical detail as to the formative influences of nature, education, and religion on Moon's early development.

In his autobiography, Moon devotes a chapter to "Loving Nature and Learning from It." He recalls at some length his boyhood adventures when he spent entire days in the hills and meadows, wandering about the forest, picking wild vegetables, climbing trees, studying birds, listening to insects, tending the family cow, aggravating hens, watching a mother pig give birth to piglets, and catching eels in water pools along a three-mile path from his home to an inlet of the Yellow Sea. He also recalls helping his older brother run the farm, plowing rice paddies and fields, transplanting seedlings, and fertilizing crops which included breaking up solid excrement by hand into small pieces. He laments that children raised in urban areas "don't have opportunities to become familiar with nature."[13]

Moon attended a traditional school in his village where he read the *Analects* of Confucius and the works of Mencius and was taught Chinese characters. However, Moon "wanted to attend a formal school, not the traditional village school." As he put it, "I felt I shouldn't be just memorizing Confucius and Mencius when others were building airplanes."[14] He and a cousin enrolled in the Unyong Institute to prepare for the exam required for admission to Osan School in Jeong-ju, the county seat, six miles away. Osan was a nationalist school where Japanese language was not taught and speaking it was forbidden. Moon was an ardent student and skipped a grade. He also learned "new subjects – Korean script, geography, history, mathematics."[15] But he disagreed with the no-Japanese policy. In his view, "[W]e had to know our enemy if we were to defeat it."[16] He took another transfer exam and entered the state-run

---

[12] M. Breen, *Sun Myung Moon: The Early Years, 1920–53* (Hurstpierpoint, UK: Refuge Books, 1997), 21.

[13] S. M. Moon, *As a Peace-Loving Global Citizen* (Washington, DC: The Washington Times Foundation, 2009), 38.

[14] Ibid., 41. [15] Breen, 30. [16] Moon, *As a Peace-Loving Global Citizen*, 42.

Jeong-ju Public Normal School, memorizing the Japanese katakana and hiragana alphabets before his first day at the school.

Moon's entire family converted to Christianity in 1930. According to him, this occurred "by the grace of Great-Uncle MOON Yun-guk, who was a minister and led a fervent life of faith."[17] MOON Yun-guk, who had beguiled the family into donating their fortune to the Korean government in exile, converted to Christianity in 1910, graduated from Union Theological Seminary, Pyongyang in 1918, and pastored three local Presbyterian churches. However, Breen reports that the family's conversion was precipitated by faith healings of Moon's elder sister and brother.[18] Whatever the circumstances, Moon took to the new faith with zeal. He reports,

> I attended church faithfully, without ever missing a week. If I arrived at service even a little late, I would be so ashamed that I could not even raise my face. I don't know what I could have understood at such a young age to inspire me to be this way, but God was already a huge presence in my life.[19]

Moon became increasingly preoccupied with questions of life and death. At the age of twelve, he reports witnessing his great-grandfather's grave being moved and viewing his remains, which filled him with "shock and fear."[20] At fifteen, five of his younger siblings died in a single year. To him, "The suffering of one family seemed connected to the suffering of the nation and of the world. I was increasingly troubled to see the wretched situation of the Korean people under Japan's increasingly tyrannical rule."[21]

This raised in his mind the question of theodicy, why tragic events happen to good people. He clung to religion, but as he expressed it,

> The Word of God I was hearing in church ... was not sufficient by itself to give me the clear answers I was seeking. To relieve the frustrations in my heart, I naturally began to immerse myself in prayer ...
> Prayer helped me to find solace. Whenever I laid out the anguishing problems in my heart to God, all my suffering and sorrow vanished and my heart felt at ease. I began spending more and more time in prayer, to the point that, eventually, I began praying through the night all the time.[22]

This, in turn, led to a life-altering experience. Moon testifies that the night before Easter in the year he turned sixteen, he "was on Mount Myodu praying all night and begging God in tears for answers."[23] Then, early on Easter morning, after spending the entire night in prayer, he recounts that Jesus appeared before him,

---

[17] Ibid., 46.   [18] Breen, 28.   [19] Moon, *As a Peace-Loving Global Citizen*, 46–47.
[20] Ibid., 47.   [21] Ibid., 48.   [22] Ibid., 49.   [23] Ibid.

He appeared in an instant, like a gust of wind, and said to me, "God is in great sorrow because of the pain of humankind. You must take on a special mission on earth having to do with Heaven's work."

That day, I saw clearly the sorrowful face of Jesus. I heard his voice clearly. The experience of witnessing the manifestation of Jesus caused my body to shake violently, like a quaking aspen's leaves trembling in a strong breeze. I was simultaneously overcome with fear so great I felt I might die and gratitude so profound I felt I might explode. Jesus spoke clearly about the work I would have to do. His words were extraordinary, having to do with saving humanity from its suffering and bringing joy to God.[24]

Moon states that his initial response was, "I can't do this. How can I do this?" He describes himself as "truly afraid," wanting somehow to avoid the mission, noting that he "clung to the hem" of Jesus' clothing and "wept inconsolably."[25]

In his autobiography, Moon recounts that the Easter encounter threw him into extreme confusion. He felt he could not share his "huge secret" and "was at a loss over what to do."[26] He recognized this would require him to sacrifice the rest of his youth and acknowledged "foolish thoughts," feeling at times that he "would rather avoid the path."[27] Nevertheless, over the next decade he consciously expanded the scope of his activity. During the summer following his Easter experience he undertook a pilgrimage around the country which confirmed that Korea was "a crucible of tears" and redoubled his "determination toward my future work."[28] He testified to Jesus' ongoing appearances and began separating himself from conventional expectations. In 1938, on the day of his graduation from Jeong-ju Public Normal School, he delivered a student address in which he referred to each of his teachers by name, criticizing them and "pointing out problems in the way the school was run."[29] He also declared, "Japanese people should pack their bags as soon as possible and go back to Japan." He noted, "From that day, the Japanese police marked me as a person to be tracked and began watching me, making a nuisance of themselves."[30]

From 1938–41, Moon attended Kyongsong Institute of Commerce and Industry, a middle school for boys run by a Japanese headmaster in the Heuksok district of Seoul. Adopting the motto, "Before seeking to dominate the universe, first perfect your ability to dominate yourself," he ate two meals a day, lived in an unheated lodging, cut the hair of beggars under the Han River bridge, and prayed for hours in his lodging and on a small hill nearby.[31] He attended a Pentecostal church and then the Myungsudae Worship Hall, the Seoul branch of the New Jesus Church. The Myungsudae Worship Hall had been founded by the noted Korean mystic and revivalist LEE Yong-do

---

[24] Ibid.   [25] Ibid., 50.   [26] Ibid., 51.   [27] Ibid., 53.   [28] Ibid., 55.   [29] Ibid., 43.
[30] Ibid.   [31] Ibid., 57, 62–63.

(1900–33), who was expelled from the Methodist Church in 1932, and BAEK Nam-ju, a controversial figure who had been expelled from the Presbyterian Church for messianic teachings.[32] Moon served as a Sunday School teacher, taught Bible lessons, evangelized, and spoke to peers about Korea as the "second Israel."[33]

Moon dramatically expanded the scope of his experience by enrolling as a student at Waseda Koutou Kougakko, a technical engineering school affiliated with Waseda University in Tokyo, Japan, which he attended from 1941–3. He traveled there under the Japanese name, EMOTO Ryumei.[34] At Waseda, he studied electrical engineering because he felt he "could not establish a new religious philosophy without knowing modern engineering."[35] He recounts always having three Bibles open on his desk, in Korean, Japanese, and English. He poured over them, underlining verses and making notes in the margins until the pages "became stained with black ink and difficult to read."[36] He also researched books on religion, brought home philosophy books, argued with Korean communist students, and began systematizing his ideas. Notably, he became active in the Korean student underground independence movement. He reports being under surveillance, stating he "cannot even remember the number of times" he was "taken into custody by the police, beaten, tortured, and locked in a cell."[37]

Due to the Second World War, Moon graduated six months early on September 30, 1943. As an engineering graduate, he was exempt from active military duty but required to find work with a company contributing to the war effort.[38] He took a job in the electrical department with Kashima-gumi Construction Company, Seoul. He married CHOI Sun-gil (b. 1925) on May 4, 1944. In his autobiography, Moon notes that he "came to feel intuitively that the time had come for me to marry."[39] Elsewhere, he states that he married "in accordance with Heaven's Will" and that his wife was a "model Christian."[40] They began married life in his boarding room at Heuksok Dong, and Moon continued his church work with the Myungsudae Jesus Church. If Moon's life had taken a conventional turn, it was interrupted in late 1944 when Japanese police arrested him because a friend from Waseda, who was accused of being a communist, mentioned his name. Moon insisted he was a Christian and described in graphic detail the tortures he endured after he was arrested. These included being beaten while hung from the ceiling "like a slab of meat

---

[32] Breen, 42–45.
[33] K. Park, "True Father Was My Sunday School Teacher" (July 13, 2016), www.tparents.org/Library/Unification/Talks/Park/Park-160713.pdf, accessed December 2, 2021.
[34] Breen, 48.   [35] Moon, *As a Peace-Loving Global Citizen*, 67.   [36] Ibid.   [37] Ibid., 68.
[38] Breen, 62.   [39] Moon, *As a Peace-Loving Global Citizen*, 80.
[40] S. M. Moon, "First Months Back in Korea," *Today's World* 29, no. 4 (May 2008): 9.

hanging in a butcher shop" and being forced to swallow water until bloated, laying face up on the floor, while police stomped on his abdomen with their military boots.[41] On the days afterward, Moon notes, "I had no energy and would just lie face down on the floor, completely unable to move."[42] He was released in February 1945.

Moon's Early Ministry

Japan's August 15, 1945 surrender marked the beginning of Moon's public ministry. Over the next nine years, he sought to gain followings in Seoul (1945–6), Pyongyang (1946–8), and Pusan (1951–3). In the North, he was jailed from 1948–50. During this period, he had marginal success in gaining followings but succeeded in consolidating his teaching and setting the foundations for what would become the Unification Church.

Moon writes that he could not join in the general jubilation following Korea's liberation from Japan as he sensed looming calamities facing the nation.[43] Initially, he attempted to connect with mainline churches and nascent political parties. This was extraordinarily difficult amid the postwar chaos. Korean Christianity was weakened by rifts over Shinto shrine worship and rival political factions were distracted by violent infighting. By this time, Moon had solidified his sense of messianic identity and turned to spiritual groups who expected the Lord's return in the flesh. In late 1945, he connected with the Israel Monastery, an offshoot of the New Jesus Church. It was a small group but included among its congregation the wife of the owner of Korea's main daily newspaper, the *Chosun Ilbo*, and the wife of LEE Bom-sok, who became South Korea's first prime minister in 1948.[44] Moon worked with the group for six months. However, he failed to win over its leader, KIM Baek-moon, and decided, "I had to go my own way."[45]

Moon arrived in Pyongyang on June 6, 1946. In his autobiography, he describes his departure from Seoul as the result of a sudden revelation,

> We ran out of rice in our home, so I set out for Paekchon, Hwanghae Province, a community north of Seoul and just south of the 38th parallel, to pick up some rice that had been purchased previously. On my way, though, I received a revelation that said: "Go across the 38th parallel! Find the people of God who are in the North."
>
> I immediately crossed the 38th parallel and headed for Pyongyang. It had been only a month since our first son was born. I was concerned for my wife. I knew she would be anxiously waiting for me, but there was no time for me to

---

[41] Moon. *As a Peace-Loving Global Citizen*, 83.   [42] Ibid.   [43] Ibid., 85.   [44] Breen, 67–68.
[45] S. M. Moon, "Liberation and Aftermath," *Today's World* 29, no. 7 (August 2008): 9.

return home before going north. God's commands are very serious, and they must be followed without reservation or hesitation.[46]

Elsewhere, Moon states that churches in the South had set his wife against him. As he explained it, "She and her mother united in their opposition ... saying, 'Whoever says the Lord will come in the flesh is an enemy, the Antichrist'."[47] Whatever his motivation in crossing into the North, he had taken a radical step, transgressing conventional norms. It would be more than six years before he saw his wife and child again.

Moon's Pyongyang ministry advanced beyond his earlier activity in that he actively sought followers and led an independent congregation. Critics of his followers were spiritualists and many came from still flourishing mainline churches. However, a combination of aggressive proselytizing and noisy services led to complaints. On August 11, 1946, police took Moon into custody, charging him with being a spy from the South and using religion to deceive people. In prison, Moon met members of the Inside-the-Belly Church, a messianic sect whose female leader's womb shook when receiving revelations, indicating that Christ would return in the flesh. Moon's note to her, asking that she deny her revelations in order to be released and to pray about the one who sent the note, was found by prison guards and resulted in his severe torture. He was released on November 21, 1946 and nursed back to health by followers. Huн Ho-bin, the Inside-the-Belly Church leader, refused to disavow her revelations and later died in prison.[48]

Moon continued to preach and build his congregation. In 1947, he attempted without success to convert Pak Eul-ryong who referred to herself as the "Wife of Jehovah" and led a messianic group, *Kwang-ya Kyohae* ("Wilderness Church") in Pyongyang.[49] Critics claim that during this period and afterwards Moon engaged in p'ikareum ("blood separation" or "cleansing of the womb"), a form of ritual sex alleged to be practiced by Korean messianic sects in the 1940s and 1950s.[50] However, in the *Advent of Sun Myung Moon*, George Chryssides concludes, "there is no evidence to support the allegation that the UC ever engaged in this practice," and he further states, "it cannot even be established that the Rev. Moon had contact with any Korean religious groups who may have practiced the ritual of p'ikareun."[51] Moon was again arrested on

---

[46] S. M. Moon, *As a Peace-Loving Global Citizen*, 86.

[47] S. M. Moon, "Liberation and Aftermath," 7.   [48] Breen, 77–80.

[49] S. M. Moon, "The Difficulty of Undoing the Reversal of Dominion," *Today's World* 29, no. 10 (November–December 2008): 9–11.

[50] K. Nevalainen. *Change of Blood Lineage through Ritual Sex in the Unification Church* (Charleston, SC: BookSurge Publishing, 2010).

[51] G. Chryssides, *The Advent of Sun Myung Moon* (London: Palgrave Macmillan, 1991), 106, 132.

February 22, 1948, this time charged with disrupting the social order. A follower at the time claimed Christian ministers sent some eighty letters to communist authorities denouncing him.[52] He was tried on April 7 before communist officials and Christian pastors, mocked with questions about how he came to earth, and sentenced to five years imprisonment at Hungnam labor camp.

Moon arrived at Hungnam on May 20, 1948. It was located on Korea's east coast to minimize escape attempts and visits from relatives of prisoners, such as Moon, from western provinces. Hungnam's nitrogen fertilizer factory provided fertilizer to the Soviet Union in exchange for weaponry. Grouped into teams of ten, prisoners were required to fill 1,300 bags of ammonia sulfate daily, each weighing 40 kilograms (88 lbs.), from 20-meter high solidified mounds.[53] Conditions were atrocious, comparable to Soviet gulags: starvation diets, unheated barracks, tattered clothing, a lack of sanitation, rampant disease and death, and compulsory propaganda sessions. Following the outbreak of the Korean War on June 25, 1950, massive sorties of B-29 bombers pounded the Hungnam industrial complex in late July and early August. Moon survived the sea of fires and executions of prisoners. On October 13, 1950, having previously retaken Pyongyang, United Nations (UN) ground forces advanced on Hungnam. Guards abandoned their posts, the gate was left open, and Moon notes, "at around two o'clock in the morning on the next day I walked calmly out."[54]

It took Moon ten days to make his way across the peninsula to Pyongyang. There, he spent forty days recovering and searching for members of his congregation, most of whom were scattered by the war or had lost confidence in him. During that period, the Chinese Red Army entered the war and was driving UN troops southward, closing in on Pyongyang. The city was ablaze, with ammunition dumps being exploded and records burned. Orders came to evacuate, and on December 3, 1950 Moon departed with one disciple, KIM Won-pil, and a follower from Hungnam, PAK Chong-hwa.

Abandoning the main roads which were blocked by retreating troops and military equipment, they traveled by narrow paths and over abandoned rice fields. Making matters worse, Pak had previously sustained a broken leg which required Moon and Kim to take turns pushing and pulling him on a bicycle. Staying in abandoned houses and scavenging for food, they made it to Seoul on December 25, 1950. However, there was little time to pause as the Chinese and

---

[52] W. P. Kim, "Father's Early Ministry in Pyongyang," *Today's World* 3, no. 1 (January 1982): 19.

[53] S. M. Moon, "Pyongyang Prison, Hungnam Labor Camp," *Today's World* 30, no. 2 (March 2009): 8.

[54] S. M. Moon, *As a Peace-Loving Global Citizen*, 106.

North Korean armies were approaching. United Nations troops pulled out of Seoul on January 3, 1951 and the city changed hands for a third time during the war. Moon, Kim, and Pak continued their journey south, careful to avoid village patrols searching for communist infiltrators. Pak, who had almost recovered, accepted an offer to stay in Gyeongju. Moon and Kim continued, traveling the last 50 kilometers by train from Ulsan to Pusan at the southeastern tip of the Korean peninsula. Breen writes, "As there was no room in the passenger coaches, they rode up front, clinging on to the front of the engine, the warmth of the steam engine on their backs and a biting winter wind freezing their faces. They arrived at Choryung Station in Pusan, cold and hungry, on January 27, 1951."[55] It had taken nearly two months to reach Pusan from Pyongyang.

Moon and Kim lived the life of refugees in Pusan. They struggled to find food and shelter. However, they met acquaintances from the North and eventually their lives stabilized. Kim worked as a waiter and later as an assistant painter on an American army base. He did portraits of soldiers' wives, girlfriends, and family members on the side. Moon worked on the docks. In July 1951, they moved to a hillside district on the edge of the city where they constructed a primitive hut. They leveled out a foundation, built walls of mud and rock, and a roof of cardboard boxes. Moon described it the "worst house" in Pusan.[56] A lady evangelist who became his first convert remembered her reaction on visiting: "I thought that if anybody had to live in such a house, he would be filled with resentment for the rest of his life."[57] Nevertheless, it was there that Moon completed a handwritten manuscript of his teaching, *Wolli Wonbon* (original text of the *Divine Principle*, unpublished).

Moon began working on the text in May 1951, but the laborers' quarters where he was staying were loud and not conducive to writing. He undertook the task seriously on the hillside of Pomne-gol and finished the manuscript on May 10, 1952. The manuscript's organization, particularly its later published version, resembled *The Fundamental Principle* (1958), by KIM Baek-moon, leader of the Israel Monastery where Moon served for six months. However, Breen cites PAK Sang Ne, a member of KIM Baek-moon's group for twenty-seven years and later a theologian at Yonsei University, who observed, "the two men's teachings, although superficially similar in categories, are very different in content."[58] As noted, messianic, spirit-led groups in the 1930s and 1940s taught that the Lord would return to Korea as a man in the flesh, that the original sin was fornication, that Jesus should not have been crucified, and that the

---

[55] Breen, 137.

[56] S. M. Moon, "Refugee Life," *Today's World* 30, no. 6 (September–October 2009): 7.

[57] H. S. Kang, "From Evangelist to Disciple," *Today's World* 3, no. 8 (August 1982): 17.

[58] Breen, 185.

returning Lord would establish a new blood lineage. Moon understood these views to be preparatory for his teaching and role.

On the day he finished writing *Wolli Wonbon*, Moon wrote, "I put my pencil down and prayed, 'The moment has come for me to evangelize'."[59] However, the work was painfully slow. Curious people made the trek up the hillside to hear the young man making preposterous claims, but few returned. Moon was able to reunite with several "grandmothers" who had been with his ministry in Pyongyang, a classmate from his student days in Japan, and the daughter of his former landlord in Seoul. KANG Hyun-shil, the lady evangelist who visited his hut, became a follower as did LEE Yo-han, a former Presbyterian minister. A turning point came with the signing of the Korean Armistice on July 27, 1953. Despite the war's lingering effects, the end of hostilities introduced a feeling of optimism which benefited the tiny group. A week before the signing, Moon sent KANG Hyun-shil to pioneer Taegu, 60 miles to the north of Pusan. He sent LEE Yo-han to join her in August. They were able to establish a beachhead and on September 17, 1953 Moon moved to Seoul. EU Hyo-won, who later became Unification Church president, and three of his brothers joined Moon's incipient group in Pusan. KIM Sang-chul, a South Korean government official, became a member in Taegu. Both joined Moon in Seoul.

Work expanded but was hindered by opposition from Christian churches and the family members of converts, similar to the dynamic in Pyongyang. Moon noted his name became "synonymous with heresy and pseudo-religion." Chased by opponents, Moon recalled, "There was one month in Taegu when I had to move thirteen times."[60] Breen reports that in March 1953, Moon formally changed his name from Yong-myung to Sun-myung "because Christians could use the name Yong, which means 'dragon,' as evidence that Moon was the antichrist." Another reason was "to avoid the families of members, who were pestering the police to arrest him."[61] However, Moon's most serious family problem was his own. On a cold, windy day in November 1952, his wife and now six-and-a-half-year-old son arrived at the door of the Pomne-gol hut. She had acquired directions from one of Moon's cousins while working in the Pusan international market. She and Moon made efforts to reunite, but it was impossible for her to integrate with the small community. She neither understood nor accepted Moon's ministry. For his part, Moon acknowledged, "I was not yet to the point where I could take care of my family."[62] There were several ugly scenes that included her cursing members and driving them out. When Moon relocated to Seoul, she remained behind in Pusan.

---

[59] S. M. Moon, *As a Peace-Loving Global Citizen*, 118.

[60] S. M. Moon, "The Months before the Founding of Our Church," *Today's World* 30, no. 7 (November 2009): 12.

[61] Breen, 158.   [62] S. M. Moon, *As a Peace-Loving Global Citizen*, 120.

3 Holy Spirit Association for the Unification of World Christianity (HSA-UWC), 1954–1994

Sun Myung Moon and four followers founded the Holy Spirit Association for the Unification of World Christianity (HSA-UWC) in Seoul, Korea in 1954. Known as *Tongil-Kyohae*, or Unification Church (UC), the church spread to Japan in 1958 and to the United States in 1959. It sent missionaries to additional countries during the 1960s and early 1970s. The UC formally launched its world mission in 1975 when missionary teams from Japan, the United States, and Germany went to ninety-five nations. HSA-UWC was the UCM's primary designation until 1994 when Moon began referring to the Family Federation for Word Peace (FFWP), later the Family Federation for World Peace and Unification (FFWPU) as a successor entity.

The Korea Mission

HSA-UWC focused its activity in Korea from 1954 until 1972 when Moon shifted his ministry to the West and relocated to the United States. Key developments included the founding of HSA-UWC, outreach on Seoul university campuses, the stabilization of church patterns during the late 1950s, Moon's "Holy Wedding" in 1960, and the solidification of the Korean UCM during the 1960s prior to Moon's move to the United States.

Founding HSA-UWC presented a problem. Setting up a separate organization ran counter to Moon's vision of uniting Christianity and the world's religions. In his autobiography, he refutes the idea that he came to found a church.

> It was necessary to hang out a church sign, but in my heart I was ready to take it down at any time. As soon as a person hangs a sign that says "church," he is making a distinction between church and not church. Taking something that is one and dividing it into two is not right. This was not my dream. It is not the path I chose to travel.[63]

On May 2, 1954, Moon gathered four followers and proposed the new association. According to one of the signatories, its objectives were: "To unite all the scattered Christian denominations throughout the world without initiating a new Christian denomination, and based on the unification of world Christianity, to bring unity among all past and present major religions to build the Kingdom of Heaven on earth."[64] The following day, they hung a signpost

---

[63] S. M. Moon, *As a Peace-Loving Global Citizen*, 123.
[64] D. Kim, "My Early Days in the Unification Church," *Today's World* 6, no. 1 (January 1985): 24.

outside a ramshackle residence with two tiny rooms and a small kitchen known as The House of Three Doors. Moon announced the official date of dedication retrospectively as May 1, 1954.

In Moon's eyes, the post–Second World War generation of Korean Christianity had failed. Having been rejected by Christian leaders in Seoul, Pyongyang, Pusan, and Taegu, he sought to advance his work by focusing on "second generation Christians."[65] This was the rationale for UC initiatives on the campuses of Ewha Women's University and Yonsei University. These two institutions were affiliated with the Methodist and Presbyterian churches and had close ties to mission sponsors in the United States. University students had prestige in postwar Korea and the UC concentrated efforts on both campuses, though more successfully at Ewha, beginning in October 1954.

Critical to the initiative was HSA-UWC President Eu Hyo-won's adaptation of Moon's handwritten *Principle* text into a three-day cycle of lectures. Yoon Young-yang, a relative of Eu and professor of Music at Ewha, joined in April 1954 and six months later offered her home for lectures. Han Choong-hwa, Ewha's dormitory master; Choi Won-pok, dean of students of the Faculty of Law and Political Science; and Kim Young-oon, a professor of religion who became the UC's first missionary to the United States, joined and actively proselytized for the church. Kim Sang-hee, who wrote of the ensuing controversy, estimated, "The number of Ewha students who officially joined or occasionally visited [the UC] ... [was] at least 400." He concluded, "Considering the fact that in 1955 Ewha had 4,038 students in total ... 10% of the students being attracted to the Unification Church could not have been a negligible phenomenon."[66]

In fact, the situation was explosive. In December 1954, the university pastor preached against the UC, stating, "These days, a heretic sect, so called 'Holy Spirit Association,' is running wild like a ghost. Regrettably, some twenty students of Ewha have been infected by it and even come to a point of abandoning their school. The three professors who had gone there to rescue them got also infected. How lamentable!"[67] The Ewha administration acted decisively, firing five professors and expelling fourteen students, all of whom refused to disaffiliate from the UC. Yonsei fired one professor and expelled two

---

[65] S. M. Moon, "Collision with Korean Society," *Today's World* 31, no. 1 (January 2010): 10.

[66] S. H. Kim, *The Unfinished History: The Expulsion of Fourteen Students from Ewha Womans University* (Seoul: Kookhak Jaryowon, 2015), www.tparents.org/Library/Unification/Books/EwhaHistory-180309.pdf, accessed April 11, 2022.

[67] Ibid.

students. The students went to newspapers, arguing that they were victims of religious discrimination. Several newspapers printed editorials critical of the action. Opponents effectively countered this by branding the UC a pseudo-religion and sex cult, spreading rumors that members danced in the nude. Additionally, Ewha had close connections with the South Korean government. Moon claimed that the Ministries of Education; Public Information; Internal Affairs; Justice; and Foreign Affairs collaborated with Christian leaders to "get rid" of him.[68] On July 4, 1955, police raided the church, arresting Moon and four leaders.

Moon was charged with draft evasion during the Korean War and unlawful detention of students. He was convicted of the former and sentenced to two years in prison. According to one of the Ewha students, "Christians came in droves to watch his trial" and Moon was subjected to jeering and mockery as he had been in Pyongyang.[69] The draft evasion conviction did not stand as Moon was "already beyond the age of compulsory military service" at the time of the Korean War.[70] Nevertheless, he served three months at Seodaemun Prison in Seoul before his conviction was overturned. He was released on October 4, 1955.

According to Moon, "The Yonsei–Ewha incident forced our church to the brink of destruction. The image of 'pseudo-religion,' or 'cult,' became insepar-ably identified with my name."[71] However, the UC rebounded rather quickly. Moon noted, "A year after my release from prison, our church had four hundred members."[72] Joshua McCabe, an Apostolic Church missionary, visited the UC in 1956 and reported similar numbers: "between 300 and 400" at Seoul Sunday services and eight centers from Seoul to Pusan. McCabe observed, "The fervor and sincerity of the worship, the soul stirring preaching of Mr. Moon, a born orator who stirs his congregation to response both in praying and preaching, is wonderful."[73] Growth continued. Rejected and stigmatized by religious and political elites, Moon took on the slow and laborious task of building a church from the bottom-up.

Several developments were significant. On October 7, 1955, three days after Moon's release from prison, the UC purchased its first building. Moon commented,

> We needed a place where our members could gather and offer services, so we
> took out a loan of two million won and purchased a house in poor repair on
> a hillside in Cheongpa-dong. It was one of many houses categorized then as

[68] S. M. Moon, "Collision with Korean Society," 13.   [69] S. H. Kim, *The Unfinished History*.
[70] S. M. Moon, *As a Peace-Loving Global Citizen*, 129.   [71] Ibid.   [72] Ibid., 138.
[73] J. McCabe, "Korean Report," *Apostolic Herald* (November 1956): 163–64.

"enemy property," meaning that it had been vacant since being abandoned by Japanese who left Korea at the time of our nation's liberation.[74]

He noted, "I worked with the young people of our church for four days with a sodium hydroxide solution to scrub off all the dirt."[75] Originally a Japanese temple with a moderately-sized hall, meeting and sleeping rooms, the Cheongpa-dong church served as UC headquarters and a focal point of activity for the next two decades. It enabled the UC to regularize worship services – 5 a.m., 11 a.m., and evenings on Sundays, evenings on Wednesdays – and provided a venue for daily lectures. The UC also advanced organizationally, forming the Sunghwa Students Association and publishing a monthly magazine, *Sunghwa*.

Further systematization of UC teaching was an additional growth factor. Eu Hyo-won, whose adaptation of Moon's *Wolli Wonbun* manuscript into a three-day cycle of lectures had appealed to Ehwa University faculty and students, worked with Moon to convert the lectures into a printed text. He began circulating its contents serially in *Sunghwa*. In August 1957, the UC published *Wolli Haesul* ("Explanation of the Principle"). The text enabled followers to better comprehend and articulate church teachings. The UC implemented semiannual examinations on its contents and developed training sessions for leaders.

Despite these gains, the environment for witnessing was difficult. Moon stated, "At Cheongpa-dong, like a wounded lion, we had to wait for the right time, making preparations."[76] In July 1957, members fasted for a week and went out for 40 days in twos to 120 witnessing locations throughout South Korea. Moon termed it "a new stage in the Unification Church's development."[77] Members did not openly identify themselves as members of the UC due to "vile rumors" and opposition.[78] Instead, they cleaned streets, helped in homes, and held literacy classes. They shared UC teachings and only mentioned the name of the church after building trust, but often with negative consequences. Moon visited teams in a Second World War–era jeep. Summer and winter forty-day pioneer witnessing became a UC tradition. The church sent a missionary to Japan in 1958 and two missionaries to the United States in 1959.

The UC gained traction, but Moon's marital situation was unsettled. In 1955, he agreed to a divorce which had been demanded by his wife and her family. According to Moon, she subjected members to "horrible abuse," storming into the church at all hours to curse them, destroy church property, take items

---

[74] S. M. Moon, *As a Peace-Loving Global Citizen*, 151.   [75] Ibid., 137.

[76] S. M. Moon, "The Effort Invested to Expand the Church," *Today's World* 31, no. 5 (June 2010): 15.

[77] Ibid.   [78] S. M. Moon, *As a Peace-Loving Global Citizen*, 143.

belonging to the church, even throwing "water containing human feces at members."[79] The divorce undercut or at least delayed his work. Moon taught that Jesus, as the second Adam, needed to take a bride as the second Eve so they could together serve as the True Parents to humanity. He believed he inherited that role. With the end of his marriage and protracted divorce, Moon had a relationship with KIM Myung-hee. The circumstances and nature of the relationship are obscure. They were not legally married and whether there was a church wedding is unclear. However, she gave birth to a son, MOON Hee Jin, in Japan on August 17, 1955. KIM Myung-hee had been smuggled there, ostensibly to avoid a scandal. While there, she was rumored to have been seduced or raped. She subsequently offered the child to Moon who acknowledged his paternity.[80] For the remainder of the 1950s, Moon directed his energies toward building the church foundation. MOON Hee Jin tragically died in a train accident on August 1, 1969.

On April 11, 1960, Moon married HAN Hak-ja (hereafter, Hak Ja Han), a seventeen-year-old schoolgirl. This was a shock to many in the UC, particularly those women who viewed themselves as preferred candidates. Given his previous marital experience, Moon's primary concern was that his wife should accept his mission. Hak Ja Han had been raised by a single mother, HONG Soon-ae, from the North, who was successively a member of the New Jesus Church, the Holy Lord Church, and the Inside-the-Belly Church, all forerunners to the UC.[81] She reared her daughter to have an acute sense of God as her father and regarded her role to be that of a "nanny."[82] Hak Ja Han later wrote, "I was molded from my conception to be the True Mother who would devote her life to God's purposes."[83] Moon met with Hak Ja Han and her mother for nine hours on February 26, 1960. An engagement ceremony followed at the Cheongpa-dong church on March 27 and a wedding ceremony on April 11. The day before, Moon was apprehended by the Ministry of Home Affairs on the basis of a complaint and subjected to interrogation until 11 p.m., four hours prior to the wedding which began at 3 a.m.[84]

Moon's Holy Wedding, referred to as the Marriage Supper of the Lamb, brought several changes to the UC. During the 1950s, the UC's focus was

---

[79] Ibid., 136.

[80] S. M. Moon, "Understanding the Holy Marriage Providence of Three Mothers." Speech delivered October 9, 1971, reprinted as "The Nation and Our Mission," www.tparents.org/Moon-Talks/SunMyungMoon71/SunMyungMoon-711009.pdf, accessed July 11, 2022.

[81] Chryssides, *The Advent of Sun Myung Moon*, 93–99.

[82] H. J. H. Moon, *Mother of Peace: A Memoir* (Washington, DC: The Washington Times Global Media Group, 2020), 45.

[83] Ibid., 50.

[84] S. M. Moon, "The Blessing of the True Bride and Groom," *Today's World* 31, no. 7 (October 2010): 6.

entirely religious. In the 1960s, it became a more broadly based movement, incorporating economic, cultural, and educational components with the church as its core. At the same time, the UCM continued to advance distinctively religious elements. The most important of these were Marriage Blessings with which the UCM became identified. Following his 1960 wedding, Moon blessed three couples in marriage and thirty-three the following year. The ceremonies included elaborate ritual elements, notably the reception of Holy Wine which was understood to cleanse partakers of original sin. Moon matched and blessed 72 couples in 1962, 124 couples in 1963, 430 couples in 1968 and 777 couples in 1970. In addition, the UC developed a ritual calendar, which established four major holy days (Parents' Day, Children's Day, Day of All Things, and God's Day). It also published *Wolli Kangron* (*Exposition of the Principle*, 1966), translated into English as *Divine Principle* (1973), which became HSA-UWC's official text. In 1963, HSA-UWC was legally recognized by the Korean government.

The Korean UC was impoverished during the 1950s. The only organized economic activities of note were the reselling of canceled postage stamps and the sale of hand-tinted black-and-white photographs of famous places or popular entertainment personalities. In 1962, the UC purchased an abandoned lathe used by the Japanese during the occupation, placed it in a storage room of the Cheongpa-dong church, "and called it Tongil Industries."[85] The following year, the UC launched its first boat, christened *Cheon Seung Ho* (Victory of Heaven). Machine tool production and fishing became the staples of HSA-UWC economic enterprises. By 1972, the Korean UC had established the Il Hwa Pharmaceutical Company, specializing in the production of ginseng products, and two titanium factories, producers of paints and coating materials. It also obtained a tax exemption for its Yehwa air rifles, designed for hunting birds and small animals. Tongil Industries eventually became a South Korean defense contractor. In addition, the UC acquired real estate, notably acreage bordering Cheon Pyeong Lake, northeast of Seoul – where Moon envisioned the eventual creation of a model international village – and land on Yeouido Island, Seoul, later to become South Korea's administrative and financial center which he envisioned as the future site of HSA-UWC world headquarters.

UCM diversification included cultural and educational initiatives. In 1962, Moon founded the Little Angels, a Korean children's dance troupe, as a way of introducing Korean culture overseas. Led by PAK Bo-hi, an early missionary to the United States, the troupe obtained financial backing from Lila Atchison

---

[85] S. M. Moon, *As a Peace-Loving Global Citizen*, 151.

Wallace, founder of the *Reader's Digest*.[86] By 1971, the Little Angels had performed on US national television, at the Mexico Olympic Games, the Nixon White House, the PARK Chung-hee Blue House, and in a Royal Command Performance before Queen Elizabeth II. The UCM established the Collegiate Association for the Research of Principles (CARP) in 1966 and the International Federation for Victory over Communism (IFVOC, also known simply as VOC) in 1968. Following the infiltration of thirty-one armed North Korean commandos bent on assassinating the South Korean president, Unification VOC lecturers conducted trainings for police and municipal officials.

The UCM was sufficiently developed for Moon to embark on world tours in 1965 and 1969. The 1965 tour took him to 40 nations where he set up 120 holy grounds. He took earth and stones from Korea to bury them in prayer locations where he intended to establish missions. Moon commented, "Whenever I passed through immigration on my way to and from airplanes, people thought I was a strange man because I carried around stones."[87] In 1972, Moon decided to shift the focus of his ministry to the United States. This was possible not only because of advances in Korea, but also because of work that first went forward in Japan.

Mission to Japan

Although they shared a similar cultural background, Korea and Japan had a history of enmity, notably imperial Japan's 1905–45 occupation of the Korean Peninsula. Moon grew up under the occupation and was arrested and tortured by Japanese police. The two countries did not establish diplomatic relations until 1965. Nevertheless, Japan became a HSA-UWC success story. Membership outstripped that of Korea and it became the resource engine that fueled the UCM's global advance. At the same time, *Genri Undo* or the Principle Movement, as the Japanese UC was known, sparked intense domestic opposition. This was, in part, due to Japanese distaste for things Korean; but, more importantly, it was due to the zeal with which members pursued their missions. Converts abandoned families and careers, went to war with Marxists on campuses, utilized controversial "spiritual sales methods," and intermarried with foreigners, including Koreans.

Poverty and deprivation characterized the earliest days of the UCM in Japan as it had in Korea. Several attempts to establish the mission had failed prior to

---

[86] B. Pak, *Messiah: My Testimony to Rev. Sun Myung Moon*, Vol. 1 (Lanham, MD: University Press of America, 2000), 282–83.

[87] S. M. Moon, "From Korea to the World," *Today's World* 32, no. 5 (June 2011): 10.

the work of CHOI Bong-choon (Sang Ik), who successfully established the UCM in Japan from 1958 to 1964, when he was taken by the Immigration Service and deported. Known as Reverend Nishikawa, he was raised in Japan from the age of two through his college years, and repatriated to Korea only after the Second World War. There, he converted to Christianity, smuggled himself back into Japan, and entered a Christian Holiness theological seminary. Returning to Korea, he founded an independent Holiness church. On converting to the UC in 1957, he immediately thought, "I would like to bring these words to Japan."[88] Obtaining approval from Moon, Choi again smuggled himself into Japan but was arrested by port authorities near Hiroshima on June 21, 1958. He fasted to induce illness and escaped to Tokyo from a sanatorium where he had been sent. He founded the UC on the second floor of a watch shop on October 12, 1959.

Choi had few results until he met MATSUMOTO Michiko in April, 1960. A Korean Christian whose Japanese husband had died, she became a devoted disciple. From this point onward, the UCM began to grow. A breakthrough occurred in 1962 when forty young leaders of Risshō Kōsei Kai, a neo-Buddhist sect (established in 1938), converted. While loyalty amid adversity, perseverance, and the all-or-nothing quality of Choi's example influenced converts who consciously sought to emulate his samurai pattern, more important was the Japanese affinity for organization. This was apparent in the decision to live communally in centers rather than in individual households as was the practice in Korea. The UC also worked communally. Instead of holding separate jobs, members sought common employment: first, in "haihin kaishu," the door-to-door collection of newspapers, magazines, bottles, and old clothing to be resold to junk dealers; and later, in small church-run businesses. The national church took on the qualities of a corporation. Japan was divided into eleven districts which, in turn, were separated into prefectural churches (there were thirty-six by 1966). The headquarters in Tokyo was organized into bureaus, departments, divisions, and committees. The organizational emphasis that characterized the church's structure also resulted in the creation of a systematic training program. Attaining a significantly higher level of sophistication than in Korea, programs varied in length from three to forty days at introductory or advanced levels with separate training facilities and regular staff.[89]

From its beginnings, the Japanese UCM was student-focused. Unlike the United States, where fraternities and sororities were a focus of student involvement, in Japan clubs were the center of student life. The UCM put great effort

---

[88] M. Nishikawa [S. I. Choi], "The Record of Witnessing in Japan," in *Faith and Life* (Tokyo: Kougensha, 1966), unpublished English translation.

[89] D. Giffin and B. Mikesell, "Report from Japan," *New Age Frontiers* 2, no. 2 (February 1966): 7–8.

into week-long festivals during which clubs courted members on Japanese campuses. According to a 1966 report, the National Student Movement, later known as the Collegiate Association for the Research of Principles (CARP), comprised "approximately 350 active members in 60 universities throughout Japan."[90] Following the Second World War, one of the biggest boons to the UCM and other new religious movements in Japan was the era of postwar reconstruction. Whereas Korea was still poor and the United States had achieved economic success, Japan was bustling with the excitement of economic expansion. A plethora of new religions tied into reconstruction fervor, rather than assuming otherworldly expectations. The UCM was no exception.

After 1966, the Japanese UCM faced three decades of escalating opposition. This began in 1967 with an article in *Asahi Shimbun*, one of Japan's most influential newspapers, titled, "The Religion That Makes Parents Weep."[91] Fueled by deep-rooted suspicion or even shame of anything closely connected to Korea, families of converts were particularly concerned because, unlike other Japanese new religions, the UC removed young adults from jobs, colleges, and families; sent them overseas as missionaries; and selected marriage partners regardless of family preferences. The first significant anti-UC organization, "Parents of Victims of the Unification Association," coalesced and UC members were subject to forced confinements in mental hospitals. Still, opposition was relatively isolated and ineffective. Anti-UC agitation was viewed as an issue best left for families to resolve.

A second phase erupted in 1978 when the Japanese Communist Party (JCP) declared war on the UCM. Agitated by "Victory over Communism" lectures and demonstrations on college campuses, JCP Chairman Miyamoto Kenji declared, "Stamping [out] VOC is a Historical War for Justice."[92] Articles on the UC in *Akahata* (Red Flag, the JCP's newspaper) escalated from 13 in 1975, 21 in 1976, 71 in 1977, to 1,716 in 1978.[93] The JCP fanned the flames of Japanese–Korean antagonism by claiming the UCM was founded by the Korean Central Intelligence Agency, thereby raising the specter of foreign interference. The UCM found itself cut off from programs on numerous college campuses. During the same period, anti-UC parent groups invoked brainwashing theories and adherents continued to be committed to mental hospitals or confined to makeshift cells in parents' or relatives' homes for deprogramming.

---

[90] Ibid., 9.

[91] P. Clarke, *New Religions in Global Perspective: Religious Change in the Modern World* (London: Routledge, 2006), 54.

[92] A. Hirose, *Revealed Facts of Opposing Ministers* (Tokyo: Committee of Comparative Study of Religion, 1988).

[93] I. Fukuda and T. Ueno, *The Gulag in Japan: Religious Persecution by the Communist Party* (Tokyo: Research Institute on Communism and Religious Issues, 1984).

Christian clergy often participated. Nevertheless, the UCM registered more impressive rates of growth than Christian denominations, which represented a tiny percentage of the Japanese population.

A third and more damaging phase ensued following a forty-one-page report issued by the Japanese Bar Association in 1987 against the so-called "spiritual sales method," a practice that influenced buyers through high-pressure sales tactics and fortune-telling to purchase marble vases, ivory seals, and miniature pagodas said to possess supernatural powers. Concern about salespeople preying on religious anxieties was first voiced by the Japanese Consumer Information Center, with more than 2,600 complaints lodged between 1976 and 1982.[94] The implication of UC-related businesses in the practice reinvigorated anti-UC groups, resulted in litigation and financial settlements, and increased abductions of church members. In the face of public disapproval, the UCM opened "video centers" and introduced theological teachings only after completion of non-theological preparatory video courses, a practice that was criticized as deceptive. However, Japanese UCM leaders accepted public stigmatization and deprogramming as an unfortunate but necessary price to be paid for substantial monetary and membership gains.

The Japanese UCM did not appreciably alter its profile in the 1990s or afterwards. A Japanese Victims' Association against Religious Kidnapping and Forced Conversion reported in 2013 that "roughly 4,300 followers" of the Japanese UCM had been subjected to confinement over the previous four decades.[95] The most egregious case was that of Goto Toru, held for twelve years and five months, from September 11, 1995 to February 12, 2008. He filed criminal and civil complaints and, after seven years, was awarded a 4.38 million yen (roughly US$47,000) civil judgment in 2015. This reversed the trend of Japanese courts dismissing complaints as family disputes, and effectively halted coercive deprogrammings more than thirty years after the practice had ended in the United States.

The Unification Church of Japan (UCJ) provided significant financial support for projects, particularly in the United States. In 1984, the *Washington Post* reported that the Japanese branch of the UC had "transferred at least $800 million over the past nine years" to finance UCM operations and acquisitions in the United States.[96] The UCJ continued to move millions of dollars

---

[94] J. Burgess and M. Isikoff, "Moon's Japanese Profits Bolster Efforts in U.S.," *Washington Post* (September 16, 1984): A01.

[95] M. Kamono, *Kidnapping, Confinement and Forced Conversion: A Modern Day Holocaust* (Tokyo: The Japanese Victims' Association against Religious Kidnapping and Forced Conversion, 2009), 2.

[96] Burgess and Isikoff.

a year from Japan to the United States during the 1980s, 1990s, and into the new century. In 2009, Tokyo police raided the church, arresting the president and six employees of a business allegedly related to the UC for selling personal seals for hundreds of thousands of yen and telling customers that not buying them would result in misfortune. The UCJ denied any legal or organizational connection to Happy World Inc., the main distributor of products, but acknowledged that Happy World employed its members. That put a temporary dent in sales, which was made up by followers using credit cards and even selling ancestral properties to offer donations.

For Moon, the Japanese UCM exemplified the dictum of absolute faith, absolute love, and absolute obedience. He taught that Japan is the mother nation, sacrificing herself for the world, a role the Japanese UCM embraced. Apart from donations, Japanese members were UCM frontline shock troops, prepared for mobilization globally. They engaged in extended pioneering in out-of-the-way locations such as Kodiak, Alaska, and the Pantanal in Paraguay. In 1994, Moon sent 1,600 Japanese female missionary volunteers, in teams of 10, to 160 countries throughout the world. Many left husbands and children behind. In 1996, he called on 4,200 Japanese female volunteers to undertake missionary work exclusively in South America. It was suggested that Japanese followers were motivated to "compensate for [Japan's] thirty-six year colonization of Korea."[97] In his autobiography, Moon recounts the ten-year effort of a Japanese woman to dispel the hatred of her Korean father in-law, commenting, "The daughter in-law paid for the sins of the Japanese." He described it as "an example of the path of redemption that will lead humankind into a world of peace."[98]

The United States

The UCM began work in the United States in 1959 when its first missionaries arrived in the Pacific Northwest. Its early mission extended through the 1960s up to the arrival of Moon and his wife in late 1971. During this period, fledgling groups translated core theological texts into English, established patterns of community life, and developed characteristic ways of relating to the wider society. Young Oon Kim, one of the Ewha University professors who converted in 1955, was the first to arrive, in Eugene, Oregon in January 1959. David S. C. Kim, one of the founders of HSA-UWC with Moon in 1954, was the next to arrive, in Portland, Oregon in September. Bo Hi Pak, organizer of the Little

---

[97] Y. Sakurai, "Geopolitical Mission Strategy: The Case of the Unification Church in Japan and Korea," *Japanese Journal of Religious Studies* 37, no. 2 (2010): 319.
[98] S. M. Moon, *As a Peace-Loving Global Citizen*, 222.

Angels dance troupe and a military officer, arrived in 1961, serving as assistant military attaché at the Korean Embassy in Washington, DC. Sang Ik "Papasan" Choi, who had successfully established the UCM in Japan, was the last of the original missionaries, arriving in San Francisco in late 1965.[99] Young Oon Kim incorporated HSA-UWC as a California corporation on September 18, 1961 in an effort to stabilize her residency status in the United States. Repeal of the Asian Exclusion Act in 1965 significantly aided the admission of Koreans and all Asians, including Moon, to the United States.

Young Oon Kim, or "Miss Kim" as she was known, moved to San Francisco in 1960 and then to Washington, DC in 1965 from where she led a network of centers across the country referred to as the Unified Family. David Kim established United Faith Inc. and led a string of United Chapels from the Pacific Northwest to Chicago. Bo Hi Pak set up the Korean Cultural and Freedom Foundation (KCFF) which promoted US tours of the Little Angels Korean dance troupe and later established Radio of Free Asia. Papasan Choi tapped into the communal ethos and utopian idealism of the 1960s, fashioning a communitarian experiment in San Francisco which included an International Ideal City Project on 600 acres in Mendocino County. Nevertheless, core membership of their separately incorporated groups stood at only around 300 after more than a decade of effort. But it should be noted that during the 1960s activities in the United States were peripheral to the mainstream UCM which was centered in Korea and, to a lesser extent, Japan.[100]

The UCM became prominent in the United States during the 1970s. Alienated youth, disillusioned with American society as well as with political protests and the drug culture of the 1960s, contributed to a broad constituency of religious seekers who joined the UCM and other groups. The UCM took advantage of the market opportunity by transforming itself from loosely organized, low-impact missionary groups into a unified, tightly organized, high-demand new religious movement (NRM).[101] From 1972–4, it conducted a series of "Day of Hope" evangelistic crusades in all fifty states. These culminated in a highly publicized overflow rally at Madison Square Garden in New York City on September 18, 1974 that featured Moon, with a translator, speaking on "The New Future of Christianity." Pre-rally preparations included a massive poster campaign, with ads proclaiming "September 18 Could Be Your Re-Birthday." Eighty thousand 2-by-3-foot posters with a portrait of Moon

---

[99] M. Mickler, "The Unification Church/Movement in the United States," in *Introduction to New and Alternative Religions in America*, Vol. 4, eds. E. Gallagher and M. Ashcraft (Westport, CN: Greenwood, 2006), 159.
[100] Ibid., 159–60.   [101] Ibid., 160.

wallpapered Manhattan. As reported in *The New York Times*, "His face is everywhere, it seems."[102]

These developments would have been impossible without the unifying and energizing presence of Moon. At the same time, he provided a focus for opponents. His Asian origin, alleged connections to the Korean government, and even his name afforded grist to enemies who derided followers as "Moonies" and the movement as a cult. By 1976, a broad-based anticult movement designated the UCM a primary target. Its actions put the movement on the defensive, caused it to spend millions in litigation, sparked government investigations, and generated widespread public hostility. The UCM bicentennial God Bless America rallies at Yankee Stadium and the Washington Monument in 1976, intended to close out the proclamation phase of Moon's US ministry, unfolded within a climate of widespread antagonism.[103]

Moon expected the UC to increase its core membership to 30,000 by the late 1970s in order to have a significant impact in the United States. However, that goal was exceedingly elusive. In 1973, the UCM circulated Moon's "Answer to Watergate" statement in full-page advertisements placed in most of the nation's major newspapers. In it, Moon asserted "the crisis for America is a crisis for God" and stated, "God's command at this crossroads in American history is to forgive, love and unite."[104] More than any other single factor, the UCM's well-orchestrated demonstrations in support of US President Richard Nixon catapulted it into the national spotlight. Moon secured an invitation to the 1974 annual Presidential Prayer Breakfast and a 20-minute audience with Nixon, reportedly telling him, "Don't knuckle under to pressure. Stand up for your convictions."[105] However, this guaranteed that the UCM would not only be unpopular but also scrutinized and investigated. The Immigration and Naturalization Service (now the US Citizenship and Immigration Services) denied the UC access to missionary visas and moved against the church's foreign nationals. New York City denied the church tax-exempt status. Senator Robert Dole (Republican, Kansas) convened two informal information sessions, one billed as "A Day of Affirmation and Protest," for UC critics. Congressman Donald Fraser (Democrat, Minnesota) pursued the "Moon Organization" in a 1978 congressional probe of Korean–American relations.

---

[102] E. Blau, "Sun Myung Moon, Prophet to Thousands, Stirs Waves of Controversy As He Prepares for Big Rally Here," *New York Times* (September 16, 1974): 1.

[103] Mickler, "The Unification Church/Movement in the United States," 160–61.

[104] S. M. Moon, "America in Crisis – Answer to Watergate: Forgive, Love, Unite," in *Day of Hope, in Review. Part 1, 1972–74*, ed. D. Kim (Tarrytown, NY: International One World Crusade, 1974), 178–79.

[105] L. Stern and W. MacKaye, "Rev. Moon: Nixon Backer," *Washington Post* (February 15, 1974): A1.

These developments blunted the UCM's initial surge. In 1982, the UCM conducted a record-setting wedding or Blessing for 2,075 couples at Madison Square Garden, which eclipsed the previous record of 1,800 couples married in Korea in 1975. Nevertheless UCM opponents were still active and there continued to be setbacks, notably Moon's 1981 indictment, his 1982 conviction, and his 1984–5 imprisonment on tax evasion charges stemming from anomalies in his tax returns for 1973–5.[106] According to Moon,

> During the first year I was in America, money received as donations from around the world was placed in a bank account in New York in my name, held in trust for the church, a practice common in some denominations. The funds that were in this account for three years produced interest income, and I was indicted on the charge of not paying taxes on about $7,500. Normally a fine would be charged, but I was imprisoned in the federal correctional institution in Danbury, Connecticut, on July 20, 1984.[107]

Nevertheless, during the same period, HSA-UWC obtained legal recognition in the United States as a bona fide religion with tax-exemption privileges, public solicitation rights, access to missionary visas, and protection from deprogramming.[108]

The UCM continued its witnessing and evangelization efforts during the 1980s but it did not have a sufficient number of core members to be an effective grassroots movement. As a consequence, the movement shifted its strategy, diversified, and developed an organizational infrastructure which expanded its ability to exert influence. During the 1970s, the UCM sponsored annual International Conferences on the Unity of the Sciences (ICUS), which grew to include hundreds of participants including several Nobel laureates. By then, the UCM had established active chapters of the Professors World Peace Academy (PWPA) and Paragon House which served as a publishing outlet for ICUS and PWPA-related scholars. The UCM followed a similar trajectory in ecumenical and interreligious outreach. The Unification Theological Seminary (UTS), established at Barrytown, New York with an ecumenical faculty, hosted theologians' conferences, which led to the creation of ecumenical and interreligious organizations. Hundreds of scholars of religion participated in conferences on Unification theology and related initiatives, such as the Youth Seminar on World Religions, which conducted worldwide religious pilgrimages. In 1985, the UCM sponsored an Assembly of the World's Religions in McAfee, New Jersey, which attracted 600 participants from 85 nations.

---

[106] C. Sherwood, *Inquisition: The Persecution and Prosecution of the Reverend Sun Myung Moon* (Washington, DC: Regnery Gateway, 1991).

[107] S. M. Moon, *As a Peace-Loving Global Citizen*, 186.

[108] Mickler, "No Stranger to Litigation," 80, 82–86.

The UCM also set up businesses, focused primarily on the US fishing industry. Moon noted, "The United States has three of the world's four largest fishing grounds. Three-quarters of the world's fish population live in waters near the United States. Yet, the United States has relatively few people to catch fish, and its fishing industry is extremely underdeveloped."[109] Based on this market opportunity, the UCM set up a profusion of fish-related business enterprises along the Korean *chae-bol* (conglomerate) model, acquiring shipbuilding yards in Norfolk, Virginia and Bayou La Batre, Alabama; commercial and charter fishing fleets; fish processing plants in Gloucester, Massachusetts and Kodiak, Alaska; and a nationwide distribution network consisting of wholesale and retail fish companies, restaurants, markets, and groceries. True World Foods, a UCM-related company, eventually became the leading supplier of raw fish to sushi restaurants nationwide.[110]

Work with scholars and business enterprises were long-term endeavors. The UCM garnered immediate influence by setting up *The Washington Times* in 1982. Conceived as a counterbalance to the liberal *Washington Post*, the conservative *Times* gained the endorsement of US President Ronald Reagan who reportedly read it every day.[111] As the Reagan years came to a close, the UCM became more active in public life. The UCM-related American Leadership Conference (ALC) and the American Freedom Coalition (AFC) convened American Leadership Conferences for civic leaders, distributed more than 30 million pieces of literature during the 1988 US presidential campaign, including voter scorecards, and in 1990 conducted Desert Storm rallies in all fifty states. In 1992, the PBS television series *Frontline* concluded, "Whether they know it or not, Americans should realize Rev. Moon is a force in their political lives."[112]

World Mission

The Holy Spirit Association for the Unification of World Christianity had, as its name implies, a consciousness of global mission from its inception. Missionaries were sent to Japan and the United States in the 1950s. Moon conducted world tours in 1965 and 1969, intended to increase the pace of growth. In 1975, the church greatly accelerated its global presence, sending

---

[109] S. M. Moon, *As a Peace-Loving Global Citizen*, 173.

[110] D. Fromson, "The Untold Story of Sushi in America," *New York Times Magazine* (November 5, 2021): 36–45.

[111] F. Clarkson, "Behind the Times: Who Pulls the Strings at Washington's No. 2 Daily?," *Fairness and Accuracy in Reporting* (August 1, 1987), https://fair.org/extra/behind-the-times/, accessed March 11, 2022.

[112] "The Resurrection of Rev. Moon," *Frontline*, January 21, 1992.

a wave of missionaries to more than ninety-five countries. During the 1980s, the UCM positioned itself globally through sponsorship of academic and interreligious conferences, media organizations, business enterprises, and anti-communist activities which, by the late 1980s, also included outreach to communist states.

David S. C. Kim was HSA-UWC's first overseas missionary. A Korean government official who converted in early 1954, Kim was one of the four followers with whom Moon founded HSA-UWC. In August 1954, he was selected by the Korean government to study in Britain as a UN scholar at Swansea College, University of Wales. While there, he visited churches and small groups, introduced the UC and preached its teachings. His most significant contact was Joshua McCabe, a missionary to Australia of the International Apostolic Church, a Pentecostal denomination headquartered in Wales. Kim preached at the church's world convention in South Wales, requesting aid for the then-beleaguered UC. McCabe was dispatched and arrived in Korea on June 22, 1956, spending the next eighty days with HSA-UWC leaders and members. He appreciated UC fervor and sincerity, and helped produce an English translation of *Divine Principle*. However, McCabe concluded that UC beliefs did not coincide with those of the Apostolic Church and had no further contact.[113]

The UC dispatched missionaries to Japan (1958) and the United States (1959, 1961, and 1964). Peter Koch and Paul Werner, two German nationals who joined in California, pioneered Germany and Austria, respectively, in 1963 and 1965. Teddy Verheyan, a Dutch national who likewise joined in California, pioneered Holland (1965). Their converts missionized other European countries. In 1968, Werner reported that Switzerland was the eighth European country to be pioneered. Followers missionized England, France, Italy, and Czechoslovakia from 1965–8. In 1970, representatives from seventeen European nations gathered for a continental meeting. Germany reported twelve centers in major cities.[114] Although development was haphazard and absolute numbers small, the European mission was mature enough to send 114 missionaries to the United States in 1972. Isolated missionaries, some of whom gained followings, operated between 1965 and 1974 successively in Australia, Canada, Greece, Syria, Iran, Israel, Brazil, Guyana, Mexico, Peru, Argentina, South Africa, Taiwan, Hong Kong, and New Zealand.[115]

[113] G. Chryssides, "The Welsh Connection: Pentecostalism and the Unification Church," *Religion Today* 5, no. 3 (1988): 6–8.

[114] P. Werner, "National Report on Germany." Second European Conference, Essen, West Germany, October 31–November 2, 1970, www.tparents.org/Library/Unification/Talks/Werner/Werner-701101a.htm, accessed December 6, 2021.

[115] C. H. Kwak, K. Y. Yoo, and J. H. Choe, eds., *Footprints of the Unification Movement* (Seoul: Sunghwa Publishing, 1996), 690 ff.

In February 1975, Moon announced his intention to send missionaries to 120 nations. They were to be three-person teams consisting of a Japanese, American, and German or Austrian, i.e., missionaries from former enemy nations that had prospered after the Second World War. Moon emphasized the importance of the missionaries achieving unity among themselves as a prerequisite for success in the field. He and his wife had just set a Guinness World Record with their 1,800-couple Marriage Blessing in Korea, and many of the missionaries were drawn from newly married couples. Missionary trainings began in March, and in late April and May approximately 270 missionaries left for 95 mission countries. With 30 national missions already in place, the new wave met the goal Moon set a decade earlier when he blessed 120 holy grounds worldwide. Members of the missionary "trinities" did not know one another prior to arrival, most did not speak the others' languages, and in most cases they were unfamiliar with their mission nations. A later report put it well,

> Most of these men and women had never been to the part of the world where their assigned mission country was located. Some had never heard of the country they were to pioneer. Most could not speak the local language well, and many not at all. Most even had no idea where they would stay for their first night.[116]

Despite challenges of language, culture, disease, material deprivation, and deportations, many teams won converts, established centers, and set up cottage industries to finance activities. The UCM established a world mission department in New York City with itinerant workers to oversee work, set up regional jurisdictions, began publication of an international missionary magazine, and convened conferences for missionaries and new members.

In 1980, the UCM began a clandestine, underground mission to the Soviet Union and communist nations in Eastern Europe. Begun by the Austrian national church leader Peter Koch, the project was referred to as "Mission Butterfly." Koch insisted that the missionaries publicly renounce their church membership to protect themselves and work independently of one another. Nonetheless, they were subject to surveillance, arrest, and deportation. Several years before, thirty members in Czechoslovakia had been taken into custody, one of whom died in prison.[117] Moon referred to the pain of sending members "to places where they would be watched and possibly executed for their religious activities."[118] However, by 1991, the UCM was sponsoring large-scale events and workshops in many of the same countries.

---

[116] J. Gray, "The Lessons of History Illuminate the Road to the Future," *True Peace* (June 2017): 31.

[117] J. Gray. *The Faith That Broke the Iron Curtain: The Czechoslovakia Mission under Communism* (Seoul: FFWPU International, 2019).

[118] S. M. Moon, *As a Peace-Loving Global Citizen*, 166.

After the Second World War, Moon hoped that Korean Christians would accept his Second Advent ministry. On that foundation, he believed that communism would have been eliminated, and he would have emerged on the world stage. That did not occur and he endured a self-described forty-year "wilderness course" (1945–85). By 1985, he understood himself to be in the same position as he had been at the end of the Second World War. To his mind, there was the possibility of broad acceptance and the downfall of communism. To that end, the UCM sponsored a PWPA conference in Geneva, Switzerland titled "The End of the Soviet Empire. During the same period, Moon abandoned an exclusive identification with anti-communism and coined the term "headwing" (neither right-wing not left-wing) to identify the movement's ideological stance.

Within the context of Soviet glasnost and *perestroika*, the UCM's World Media Association and the Soviet Novosti Press Agency jointly sponsored a 1990 World Media Conference in Moscow, which included a private meeting between Moon and his wife and Mikhail Gorbachev. The UCM subsequently obtained clearance to educate Soviet youth and convened the largest workshops in its history.[119] These were the result of a unique set of circumstances, but opposition followed as the Russian Orthodox Church and the Commonwealth of Independent States (CIS) took action against foreign sects. Nevertheless, the UCM had the sense that it was riding the wave of history. In December 1991, Moon met North Korean President Kim Il Sung, an encounter that the UCM interpreted as "a meeting between the world-level Jacob and world-level Esau."[120] In August 1992, the UCM convened a World Culture and Sports Festival in Seoul, conceived of as an Olympics of Culture, at which Moon declared that he and his wife were "the True Parents of humanity . . . the Savior, the Lord of the Second Advent, the Messiah."[121] In 1994, Moon began the process of reinventing the HSA-UWC as the Family Federation for World Peace and Unification.

4 The Family Federation for World Peace and Unification (FFWPU), 1994–Present

From the mid-1990s, Moon referred to the Family Federation for World Peace (FFWP) as a successor entity to the Unification Church. The vision was to create "a religious but non-sectarian membership organization for people of

---

[119] J. Baughman, "Massive Education," *Today's World* 13, no. 4 (April 1992): 20–25.

[120] B. Pak, *Messiah: My Testimony to Rev. Sun Myung Moon*, Vol. 2 (Lanham, MD: University Press of America, 2002), 322–23.

[121] S. M. Moon, "Becoming Leaders and Building a World of Peace," *Today's World* 13, no. 9 (October–November 1992): 4.

all faiths and good conscience."[122] In 1996, he formally inaugurated FFWP in Washington, DC and in 1997 added the term "Unification," making the new entity the Family Federation for World Peace and Unification (FFWPU). Because HSA-UWC was legally incorporated in multiple countries, FFWPU and HSA-UWC continued to coexist and were, for the most part, interchangeable. Nevertheless, FFWPU or "Family Federation" became the preferred designation.

Despite being conceived of as a broad-based organization, the inauguration of the FFWPU led to increasingly frank expressions of the UCM's messianic premises. In a 1995 speech delivered in multiple public venues, Moon declared: "Prominent Christians, and other leading figures of the world have only a faint idea of the forces that shape the future ... I know the direction that humankind must go, and I, with the help of God, will lead the world there."[123] This conviction underlay peace initiatives the FFWPU introduced during the middle and late 1990s. Moon subsequently proclaimed *Cheon Il Guk*, the Unification equivalent of the Kingdom of Heaven on earth, and dedicated the last years of his ministry to its realization. Following Moon's death in 2012, Hak Ja Han Moon, his widow, carved out an independent sphere of charismatic authority and carried forward the global ministry of her late husband.

Peace Initiatives

During the early 1990s, the UCM was optimistic about the prospects for imminent, substantial global transformation. To some extent, its perspective mirrored that of secular idealists who, in the wake of the West's Cold War victory, proclaimed "the end of history."[124] This optimism would be put to the test, but the UCM stayed the course and pursued an ambitious program of "world peace and unification."[125] The first component of the program was dialogue. The UCM continued to sponsor a broad array of conferences which transitioned into federations for world peace. These integrated the distinct and separate organizations of scientists, academics, media professionals, religious leaders, politicians, and civic officials that the UCM had previously established and funded. Each federation appealed to a different constituency. By the late 1990s, the UCM had instituted a dozen or more federations, i.e., the Artist

[122] T. Hendricks, "The Relation between HSA-UWC and FFWPU," HSA-UWC North America Headquarters Memo to Regional Directors, State Leaders, May 18, 1997, www.tparents.org/library/unification/talks/hendrcks/Hendricks-HSA-FFWPU.htm, accessed October 8, 2022.

[123] S. M. Moon, "True Parents and the Completed Testament Age," *Today's World* 14, no. 6 (July 1993): 11.

[124] F. Fukuyama, *The End of History and the Last Man* (New York: Free Press, 1992).

[125] Mickler, "The Unification Church/Movement in the United States," 163 ff.

Association for World Peace (established in 1995), the Federation of Island Nations for World Peace (established in 1996), the Federation of Peninsula Nations for World Peace (established in 1996), the Federation of Continental Nations for World Peace (established in 1996), and the Martial Arts Federation for World Peace (established in 1997). Moon viewed these as potential successor entities to the UN. The most spectacular launch was the Family Federation for World Peace (1996) which included speeches by former US Presidents Gerald Ford and George Bush; former President and Nobel Peace Prize winner Oscar Arias of Costa Rica; and former Prime Ministers Edward Heath (UK) and Brian Mulroney (Canada).[126]

A second component was forgiveness and reconciliation.[127] Here, the UCM derived inspiration from Moon, who worked to alter his persona from that of Cold War warrior to that of "peacemaker and unifier."[128] He also encouraged "exchange" marriages between partners from former enemy states, created situations in which followers from adversary nations worked together, and sent them out as missionary teams to the field. During the mid-1990s, the Women's Federation for World Peace (WFWP) sponsored a series of "Sisterhood Ceremonies" in Washington, DC that brought 4,000 Japanese women to be matched with an equal number of American women in 8 separate Sisterhood Ceremonies, 50 years after the end of the Second World War. These culminated in bridge-crossings in which a Japanese delegate crossed over a "Bridge of Peace" and met her American counterpart in the middle where each bowed, embraced the other, and walked down a stairwell together, hand in hand. As with the Family Federation launch, the Sisterhood Ceremonies included appearances by high-profile public figures, notably, George and Barbara Bush.[129] The FFWPU did not limit its efforts to symbolic exchanges. Members were also asked to take on sacrificial lifestyles and voluntary suffering. The group that most embodied this was Japanese women. Moon called upon them to take on an "Eve" or mother's role in the world. Japan had been funding UCM activities at significant cost for years. During the 1990s, the UCM deployed thousands of Japanese women as missionary workers. Many of them left husbands and children behind.

International Marriage Blessings were the third component of FFWPU's program of world peace and unification. Whereas the first two components

---

[126] F. Jones, "The Inaugural World Convention of FFWP," *Today's World* 17, no. 8 (September 1996): 10.

[127] Mickler, "The Unification Church/Movement in the United States," 164.

[128] J. Gavin, ed., *Reverend Sun Myung Moon: Peacemaker and Unifier* (McLean, VA: International Peace Foundation, 1990).

[129] C. Wetzstein, "Japanese and Americans Meet to Heal War's Wounds," *Today's World* 16, no. 6 (June 1995): 27–28.

dealt with conflict resolution, the sanctification of couples through the Blessing was believed to eradicate the root cause of conflict and division. Its centerpiece was the reception of Holy Wine which, in conjunction with other elements, was understood to eliminate original sin. Prior to the mid-1990s, the Blessing was a narrow gate, restricted almost exclusively to UC members. During the mid- and late-1990s, Blessings were open to anyone willing to participate. Moon had every expectation that a new messianic age was about to dawn, the most visible manifestation of which was the globalization of the Blessing. He expressed his determination to bless hundreds of thousands and even hundreds of millions of couples by the year 2000. Members went door-to-door, into the streets, in parks, on beaches, at state fairs, and other venues to "pre-bless" married couples whose unions would be sanctified by Moon and his wife at International Marriage Blessing events. The FFWPU sponsored five International Marriage Blessings between 1995–2000 in major arenas (three in Seoul Olympic Stadium, and one each in RFK Stadium, Washington, DC and Madison Square Garden, New York). With satellite links to Blessing venues worldwide, the movement claimed to have sanctified more than half a billion couples.[130]

Despite these efforts, FFWPU's program had two significant problems. One was its limited impact. Federations for World Peace and Sisterhood Ceremonies energized the UCM base but had little discernable effect on mainstream culture. What media coverage there was tended to be critical and claimed that high-profile luminaries had been bought off or deceived. International Blessings generated more coverage but introduced a second problem. Pre-blessings introduced innovations that bore only a faint resemblance to the original tradition. Rather than Holy Wine, enterprising members distributed holy lemonade to thirsty beachgoers or downtown pedestrians with little or no explanation that they were being pre-blessed. Others distributed holy candy, sometimes on automobile windshields, with printed blessing affirmations. By the end of the decade, the UCM had reached the outer limits of what was achievable or believable. Moon, himself, referred to the "devaluation of the blessing."[131]

Publicity surrounding alleged moral failings of the Moon family was an additional problem. In the early 1990s, PAK Chong-hwa, an early follower, published an especially scurrilous account in Japan entitled *The Tragedy of the Six Marys*, which alleged Moon's participation in ritual sex and asserted that his mission was to cleanse the wombs of six married women. PAK subsequently published *I Am an Apostate* in which he repudiated his charges, stating he felt

---

[130] Mickler, "The Unification Church/Movement in the United States," 164.
[131] S. M. Moon, "Let Us Perfect the Absolute Ownership and Absolute Right of Possession of God and His Children," *Today's World* 19, no. 11 (November 1998): 8.

betrayed and needed the money.[132] In 1998, Hᴏɴɢ Nan Sook, the recently divorced ex-wife of Hyo Jin Moon, the Moons' eldest son, published *In the Shadow of the Moons: My Life in the Reverend Moon's Family*. She detailed her ex-husband's drug abuse, domestic violence, and marital infidelity. She also claimed that her former father-in-law engaged in "providential affairs" and had an illegitimate son conceived after his marriage to Hak Ja Han Moon.[133] Pᴀᴋ Chong-hwa and Hᴏɴɢ Nan Sook's accounts were authored by ex-members and fit the profile of confessional apostate literature. Nevertheless, their allegations circulated widely and precipitated crises of faith and leave-taking for some.

In facing these problems, the FFWPU followed two internal tracks for its adherents. One was a spirit world ministry, which was not unprecedented. The UCM had a long-standing tradition of recourse to spiritualism, particularly in times of difficulty. During the 1980s, a young Zimbabwean member claimed to be the "returning resurrection" of Moon's deceased second son and led a short-lived worldwide revival.[134] During the 1990s, a Korean female member was understood to be the embodiment of Hak Ja Han Moon's deceased mother. With strong affinities to the Korean mudang, or female shaman tradition, Hyo Nam Kim – referred to as *Dae Mo Nim* or "Great Mother," an honorific bestowed on Moon's deceased mother-in-law – led a more enduring spiritual revival at the UCM's Cheongpyeong Lake site, in Gapyeong County, some 40 miles (about 64 km) northeast of Seoul. Dedicated to the removal of angry, resentful spirits who were seen to be interfering with members' lives and hindering the achievement of FFWPU objectives, she employed ecstatic shamanist elements, such as hour-long singing and clapping sessions to the continual beat of a bass drum. Moon authorized the revival and thousands of members, particularly from Japan, traveled to Cheongpyeong Heaven and Earth Training Center during the late 1990s, making it a major Unification pilgrimage site.

The other track was a communitarian experiment in the Brazilian and Paraguayan outback. Moon was fascinated by nature and often had members join him in primitive natural settings for physical challenges and expeditions, usually involving fishing. He believed the natural order exposed distortions of human culture and pointed the way to a more authentic existence. During the 1990s, the UCM purchased vast tracts of land in Mato Grosso do Sul, a Brazlian state, and in the Pantanal region of Paraguay. Moon established New Hope Farm

---

[132] C. Pak, "Retraction of 'The Tragedy of the Six Marys'," November 18, 1995, www.tparents .org/Library/Unification/Talks/Pak/Chung-Hwa-Pak-Retraction.htm, accessed July 12, 2022.

[133] N. S Hong, *In the Shadow of the Moons: My Life in the Reverend Moon's Family* (New York: Little, Brown and Company, 1998).

[134] M. Isikoff, "Theological Uproar in Unification Church," *Washington Post* (March 30, 1988): A1, A13.

outside the town of Jardim, Brazil (population, 21,000) as the centerpiece of its efforts. He called on Unification couples worldwide to take part in forty-day workshops in Jardim at a newly completed Educational Center for Ideal Families and World Peace. At the same time, New Hope Farm took on the character of a communitarian experiment. The UCM began construction and farming projects, and donated ambulances to towns nearby. Graduates from Unification Theological Seminary's class of 1996 were assigned as missionaries to 33 towns within a 200-kilometer radius of Jardim.

The Last Years of Sun Myung Moon's Ministry

Moon proclaimed *Cheonju Pyeonghwa Tongil Guk* (the Nation of Cosmic Peace and Harmony), abbreviated as *Cheon Il Guk*, in 2001. *Cheon Il Guk* was the Unification equivalent of the Kingdom of Heaven, and Moon viewed it as the culmination of his ministry. Previously, he had announced a fundamental shift in the order of salvation from the individual to the family.[135] *Cheon Il Guk* advanced beyond the family to the establishment of a heavenly nation. According to Moon, "*Cheon Il Guk* ... is the one nation that God loves. It is the one nation our families love. It is the one nation our clans love. It is the one nation that white, black and yellow races love."[136] He referred to the *Cheon Il Guk* era as the time during which the foundation for the heavenly nation would be set and put the UCM on a tight schedule of twelve years extending to 2013.

During this period, the FFWPU went into full-scale kingdom-building mode. In doing so, it followed two main lines of advance. The first centered on faith leaders and leaders in the public sector willing to support UCM peace initiatives. From the UCM's perspective, this was for the purpose of preparing the environment for *Cheon Il Guk*. The second line of advance differentiated *Cheon Il Guk* from anything undertaken before. Essentially, the FFWPU went about the business of birthing a nation. It registered citizens of *Cheon Il Guk*, conducted coronation ceremonies, promulgated the first articles of the constitution of the Kingdom of Heaven and constructed an "Original Palace" (*Cheon Jeong Gung*). Moon declared jubilee years, proclaimed the Era of the Pacific Rim, and instituted a new Heavenly Calendar. In short, the UCM began the process of establishing a reality that evoked and embodied its vision of ultimate order.

From the beginning of his ministry, Moon hoped to work with a representative body of clergy aligned with his Second Advent ministry. In 2000, the FFWPU invited 120 US clergy from 17 denominations, 80 percent of

---

[135] S. M. Moon, "The Reappearance of the Second Coming and the Completed Testament Era," *Today's World* 14, no. 1 (January–February 1993): 4–15.

[136] S. M. Moon, "Let Us Fulfill the Responsibility of the Third Creators," *Today's World* 22, no. 9 (November–December 2001): 10.

them African-American ministers, to Korea at FFWPU expense to set up the American Clergy Leadership Conference (ACLC). They released doves at the Demilitarized Zone, traveled to the UCM's Cheongpyeong Heaven and Earth Training Center and, in various ways, signaled support for UCM initiatives. In 2001, Moon conducted a "We Will Stand in Oneness" revival tour cosponsored by ACLC in all fifty US states. Following the tour, Moon and his wife conducted an Interfaith Marriage Blessing at the New York Hilton Hotel. Sixty-one clergy couples participated, most notably Roman Catholic Archbishop Emmanuel Milingo. Departing from his vow of celibacy, Milingo, aged seventy-one, married Maria Sung, a forty-three-year-old Korean acupuncturist and UCM follower. This sparked a firestorm of publicity, including a Roman Catholic canonical admonition, a meeting between Milingo and Pope John Paul II, his enforced separation from Maria Sung, her hunger strike at St. Peter's Square, their 2006 reunion, Milingo's excommunication, and his founding of Married Priests Now!

In 2003, Moon broke with conventional ecumenical protocol in declaring that the era of the cross was over and calling for Christian clergy to take down crosses from their churches. Based on the Unification doctrine that the crucifixion was a tragic mistake, the FFWPU set a goal of 120 crosses to be removed by US clergy on Good Friday, a total that was exceeded. One hundred and thirty-five clergy who had done so traveled to Jerusalem where they buried a wooden cross on the Potter's Field – a burial site mentioned in the Gospel of Matthew 27:7 – and took part in an ACLC-sponsored conference with a similar number of Israeli rabbis and some Muslim leaders, with whom they jointly signed a declaration, repented of mutual sins, and pledged to forgive and be reconciled with one another.[137] This began a series of Middle East Peace Pilgrimages which became a major focus of UCM activity from 2003–5. Religious leaders, civic officials, NGO leaders, professionals from various fields, and FFWPU members participated in tours that included peace walks, peace rallies, meetings with Israeli officials, and even trips to Gaza, ignoring warnings from Israeli officials.[138]

The UCM pursued a parallel track in realizing Moon's vision of renewing the UN. The UN had been a focus of Moon's attention for some time, and during the 1990s he envisioned UCM-affiliated federations for world peace as potential successor entities. In August 2000, the UCM convened "Assembly 2000" in New York prior to the UN's Millennium Summit and Millennium General Assembly. Cosponsored by the Permanent Missions of Indonesia, Uganda,

---

[137] F. Kaufmann, "Embrace of Brothers," *Today's World* 24, no. 5 (July 2003): 24–25.
[138] S. Gabb, "Going to Gaza," *Today's World* 24, no. 7 (October–December 2003): 36–40.

and Mongolia to the UN, the event afforded a platform for Moon to propose the establishment of "a religious assembly, or council of religious representatives within the structure of the United Nations."[139] Shortly afterwards, the UCM began commissioning "Ambassadors for Peace" from among its contacts, and Moon spoke of establishing an alternative UN.[140] In 2005, he founded the Universal Peace Federation (UPF) as the institutional expression of that aspiration and proposed the construction of an interhemispheric passage across the Bering Strait as a crucial link in an International Peace Highway System "connecting the world as a single community."[141]

Moon viewed Korea as the future center of global civilization, and the UCM acquired a strategic portfolio of properties, undertook impressive construction projects, and developed business enterprises, both in the South and the North. In 2005, the UCM obtained approval to develop twelve acres of land purchased thirty-five years earlier on Yeoido Island in Seoul's financial district. The development project, known as Parc1, included two office towers, one with seventy-two floors and one with fifty-six floors, a six-floor shopping mall, and an international business hotel, to be financed at a cost of US$2.1 billion. The UCM also acquired a controlling interest in a five-star JW Marriott Hotel in Seoul's metro hub, as well as in a mall complex around it known as Central City. In Yeosu, a city midway along the southern coast of Korea, the UCM broke ground on a 33-story hotel and convention center, a condominium with 280 vacation apartments, and a water theme park with a capacity for 3,000 people. It also acquired Yongpyong, Korea's largest ski resort, the site of several World Ski Cup competitions and heart-stopping scenes from *Winter Sonata*, a hugely popular 2002 Korean television drama. In the North, the UCM assumed ownership of Pyongyang's Western-style Potong Hotel, for many years the only hotel in North Korea where Western news broadcasts were available. It also entered into a joint venture with a North Korean counterpart to develop Pyeonghwa ("Peace") Motors at Nampo, thirty miles west of Pyeongyang. Beginning in 2002, it produced small cars under license from Fiat and later more diversified models from a Chinese manufacturer. The UCM obtained permission to

---

[139] S. M. Moon, "Renewing the United Nations to Build Lasting Peace," in *Renewing the United Nations and Building a Culture of Peace, A Report from Assembly 2000*, eds. T. Walsh, A. Wilson, and T. Shimmyo (New York: Inter-Religious and International Federation for World Peace, 2000), 73.

[140] M. Mickler, "Toward an Abel UN: The Unification Movement and the United Nations," *Journal of Unification Studies* 9 (2008): 49–84.

[141] S. M. Moon, "God's Ideal Family – the Model for World Peace." Keynote address delivered at the inaugural convocation of the Universal Peace Federation, September 12, 2005, www .tparents.org/moon-talks/sunmyungmoon05/SunMyungMoon-050912.htm, accessed April 12, 2022.

construct a large World Peace Center in Pyongyang, including a UCM worship hall on the top floor, which was completed in 2007.

Alongside these developments, the FFWPU pursued an internal line of advance based on Moon's proclamation of *Cheon Il Guk*. In 2001, he presided over a "Coronation Ceremony for the Kingship of God" which, as he put it, "liberated God's heart for the first time" so that "He could start His new history."[142] The FFWPU began registration workshops for members to become *Cheon Il Guk* citizens and, in 2003, Moon and his wife were crowned king and queen of Unification blessed families. Moon subsequently declared that the Sabbath had been fulfilled and that a great transition had occurred – from "the era before the coming of heaven" to "the era after the coming of heaven."[143] A 2,500-page compilation of his words, the *Cheong Seong Gyeong*, or Heavenly Scripture, was completed and translated into ten languages.

In 2006, the UCM completed construction of the Cheon Jeong Gung (Original Palace), a massive structure cut into the side of Cheon Seong Mountain overlooking its Cheongpyeong Lake Heaven and Earth Training Center northeast of Seoul. The 100,000 square-foot building included a dome, some 80 meters high, supporting 30-ton, 48-meter-high white granite columns, two semicircular wings to either side, and a plaza in front. The entire structure was modeled on the US capitol and St. Peter's Square at the Vatican. An eight-day period of festivities and an entrance ceremony marked it as the *Cheon Il Guk* capitol. The *Cheon Il Guk* flag, national anthem, national flower, and national bird were adopted and a Peace Kingdom Corps and Peace Kingdom Police were inaugurated. Some 5,000 participated in the entrance ceremony and as many as 25,000 viewed it from video screens set up in different areas of the Cheongpyeong complex.

Moon declared a "Great Jubilee Year" in 2007 and extended it through 2008. He envisioned the rise of a Pacific Rim era, centered on the Korean peninsula. In late 2008, the FFWPU began Original Divine Principle workshops, later retitled Original Substance of Divine Principle workshops. These supplemented UCM teachings with practical content related to living in the Kingdom of Heaven and theological content explicating the relationship between the eternal Godhead, transcendent of time and space, and Moon and his wife as the "Parents of Heaven, Earth and Humankind."[144] In 2010, Moon introduced a new Heavenly Calendar, essentially the same as the lunar calendar, apart from beginning with year one. Internal communications designated dates according to the Heavenly Calendar, with Gregorian calendar dates in parenthesis. Moon also prepared his "last words

---

[142] S. M. Moon, "The Kingdom of Heaven: Who Will Enter It, and How Will They Get There?" *Today's World* 22, no. 2 (February 2001): 9.

[143] S. M. Moon, "Declaration of *Ssang Hab Shib Seung Il*," *Today's World* 25, no. 4 (June 2004): 10.

[144] H. J. (Sean) Moon, "The Messianic Identity," *Today's World* 33, no. 1 (January 2021): 1, 13–17.

to humankind" in the form of "Eight Great Textbooks." These included his collected sermons, *Exposition of the Divine Principle*, and the *Cheong Seong Gyeong* (Heavenly Scripture) among others.[145]

Moon's proclamation of *Cheon Il Guk* and what followed were instances of theological prolepsis, the anticipation or representation of future events. The initiatives mobilized the UCM base and propelled it forward. However, Moon remained suspect and despised or feared by outsiders. In 1995, Germany identified Moon and his wife as "dangerous persons," banning them from entering the country. Britain banned Moon but not his wife the same year. Germany's ban, normally applied to criminals and terrorists, was followed by most Western European nations, forcing the FFWPU into a twelve-year legal battle to reverse them.[146] Moon, himself, continued to be provocative, often intentionally. Apart from marrying a Roman Catholic archbishop, he and his wife blessed 120 young international couples in a UN conference room, an action that UN officials viewed as a "serious breach of the rules for use of UN facilities."[147] In 2002, he directed the FFWPU to publish "A Cloud of Witnesses: The Saints – Testimonies to the True Parents" in a full-page ad space purchased from leading newspapers in all fifty US states. It purported to be professions from the spirit world by Jesus, the twelve apostles, and numerous figures from Christian history; Confucius, Buddha, Muhammad and their followers; and four representative communist leaders (Marx, Lenin, Stalin, and Deng Xiao Ping). They all testified to Sun Myung Moon as "the Savior, Messiah, Second Coming and True Parent of all humanity" and the "Unification Principle" as "a message of peace for the salvation of humanity."[148] The most striking provocation was a 2004 Ambassador of Peace awards banquet in the Dirksen Senate Office Building in Washington, DC at which Moon and his wife, dressed in royal regalia, were presented with crowns of peace by an African-American congressman and White Christian pastor.[149]

The FFWPU worked to limit the fallout after each of these messianic provocations. Its efforts, at least with nonmember supporters, were generally

---

[145] S. M. Moon, "Cosmic Assembly for the Settlement of the True Parents of Heaven, Earth and Humankind and for the Proclamation of the Word by God's Substantial Self." Speech delivered at public rallies, Republic of Korea, January 8–15, 2012, www.tparents.org/Moon-Talks/SunMyungMoon12/SunMyungMoon-120108b.htm, accessed December 10, 2021.

[146] M. Vasmatics, "Breaking the Twelve-Year European Ban against Rev. and Mrs. Sun Myung Moon," *Journal of Unification Studies* 22 (2021): 133–52.

[147] H. Payne and B. Gratzer, "Rev. Moon and the United Nations: A Challenge for the NGO Community," Global Policy Forum, November 2001, https://archive.globalpolicy.org/ngos/credib/2001/1101moon.htm, accessed March 12, 2022.

[148] Y. S. Kim, "A Cloud of Witnesses: The Saints – Testimonies to the True Parents" (July 4, 2002), www.tparents.org/Library/Unification/Talks/Kim/Kim-CloudOfWitness.htm, accessed March 12, 2022.

[149] S. Stolberg, "A Crowning at the Capital Creates a Stir," *New York Times* (June 24, 2004): A17.

successful. Most were familiar enough with UCM premises so that messianic expressions were neither unexpected nor unsettling. Some were veterans of earlier controversies who remained supportive through waves of negative publicity. However, more significant than outside criticism were fissures that opened, or were exposed, within the UCM. One of these was a Korean–American divide. For example, Korean leadership interpreted the Dirksen Senate Office Building event as America "surrendering to True Parents in the king position,"[150] whereas American leadership was at pains to argue that Moon did not wish to unite church and state and that neither he nor the movement had any interest in temporal power. Another fissure was a progressive–conservative divide. Despite the UCM's long association with social and political conservativism, Moon was a globalist with a vision of economic equalization and environmental protection. These ideals were not embraced by segments of UCM membership that favored a strong national defense, unfettered capitalism, protection of private property, and aggressive development of natural resources. Korean–American and progressive–conservative tensions were long-standing within the UCM. A new fissure, which became a fracture, was a divide that opened up among Moon's adult children, now leaders, over whether the FFWPU should identify as a movement or a church.

Moon's eldest living son, Hyun Jin (Preston), was an unyielding advocate of the FFWPU as a movement. In 2008, he wrote, "The Unification Movement must get rid of its church-centered framework" and be "an inter-religious, international, interracial movement that can unite all religions, nations and NGOs within the 'One Family Under God' . . . peace movement."[151] He leveraged his position as vice president of FFWPU International and vice-chair of the UPF to convene a series of Global Peace Festivals (GPFs) in diverse international locales. Opposition came from his siblings – Kook Jin (Justin) Moon, who chaired the UCM's Tongil Group enterprises in Korea; Hyung Jin (Sean) Moon, who was elevated to international president of the FFWPU; and In Jin (Tatiana) Moon, who led a megachurch styled Lovin' Life Ministry in the United States. They considered GPFs a waste of resources and argued that the FFWPU needed to build up its material assets, professionalize its organizational structure, and dramatically increase core membership in order to influence society. This led to Hyun Jin Moon's departure in 2009 and lawsuits over UCM assets that he controlled (see Section 5).

---

[150] T. Walsh, "Notes concerning Father's Comments and Rev. Kwak's Guidance concerning the Crown" (2004), www.tparents.org/UNews/Unws0404/coron_tf_kwak_notes.htm, accessed March 12, 2022.

[151] H. J. Moon, "Report to Parents" (March 23, 2008), www.tparents.org/Moon-Talks/HyunJinMoon/HyunJinMoon-080323.htm, accessed March 13, 2020.

As troubling as these developments were, the FFWPU's core ministry continued to be that of Sun Myung Moon. He did not alter his approach in response to movement turmoil, his adult children's emerging ministries, or his advanced age and physical decline. In fact, he maintained a daily schedule that taxed attendants to keep pace. He remained wholly focused on his vision of *Cheon Il Guk* and Foundation Day, intended to mark its launch. However, he became ill with a viral infection, it worsened, and he died unexpectedly due to complications from pneumonia on September 3, 2012. This was just prior to the 2013 Foundation Day target date toward which he and the UCM had focused their efforts since 2001. Amid the resultant uncertainty, Hak Ja Han Moon, his widow, made it clear that she would carry on his ministry to Foundation Day and beyond.

The Ministry of Hak Ja Han Moon

Hak Ja Han Moon consolidated her position as leader of the FFWPU after Moon's death. She was a seventeen-year-old schoolgirl when she married Sun Myung Moon in 1960. Over time, she won the respect of members for her dedication to her husband, for her grace and charm, and for having borne fourteen children. Nevertheless, her public activities were limited. As chair of the Women's Federation for World Peace, she delivered hundreds of keynote addresses at UCM-sponsored rallies and speaking tours during the 1990s and afterward.[152] Moon referred to her as the UCM's cofounder or "second founder."[153] Nevertheless, her rise to leadership was not assured. She faced opposition, notably from two of her sons, both of whom regarded themselves Moon's rightful successor. They discounted her leadership claims, favored male-dominant models of UCM leadership, and attacked her initiatives as a desecration of their father's legacy. Both siphoned off members into breakaway organizations. Despite this, Hak Ja Han Moon retained control of the FFWPU and the vast majority of its members.

Moon's endorsement was important, but Hak Ja Han Moon's statements and actions were more consequential in establishing her authority following his death.[154] In a public address delivered two days after her husband's *seonghwa* (funeral), she stated, "I want to make clear that I shall inherit True Father's

---

[152] M. Mickler, "The Post-Sun Myung Moon Unification Church," in *Revisionism and Diversification in New Religious Movements*, ed. E. Barker (Farnham, UK: Ashgate, 2013), 58.

[153] S. M. Moon, "Parents Day and I," *Today's World* 11, no. 5 (May 1990):9.

[154] M. Mickler, "Gender Politics in the Post-Sun Myung Moon Unification Movement," in *The Life and Legacy of Sun Myung Moon and the Unification Movements in Scholarly Perspective*, ed. C. Vonck. Acta Comparanda, Subsidia VI (Antwerp: Faculty of Comparative Religion and Humanism [FVG], 2018), 204–13.

victorious foundation and stand in the forefront to lead the providence on earth."[155] A week later, in a message sent to regional headquarters and mission nations, she announced, "Everything that is carried out in Korea from this day onward will be centered on True Mother."[156] She immediately took action to ensure that would indeed be the case by dismantling the FFWPU's Korean headquarters led by her youngest son, Hyung Jin (Sean) Moon. She directed him to head the American UCM, thereby removing him from Korea as well as his duties as international FFWPU president. She subsequently moved the FFWPU Korean and international headquarters to the UCM's Cheonpyeong Lake Heaven and Earth Training Center and took over direct supervision of the international movement.

A second dimension of Mrs. Moon's leadership assertion was her critique of the way things had been done previously in the UCM. In speeches inaugurating the Women's Federation for World Peace during the 1990s, she contrasted "the masculine logic of power" with the "feminine logic of love."[157] After Moon's death, she extended her binary critique to Unification culture, questioning whether "women had been treated well by their children and husbands."[158] She expressed determination to make the UC a church "increasing with new members" and "filled with vitality."[159] She listed evangelism and youth education as top priorities and moved with surprising speed to deconstruct projects begun by her late husband. Within three months of his death, she sold the helicopter Moon had used, discontinued costly biennial soccer tournaments the UCM had sponsored since 2003, and jettisoned Pyeonghwa Motors, the North Korean auto plant into which the UCM had invested millions. She testified to her husband's ongoing presence and consent but was prepared to incorporate her distinctive experience and insights. She described her ministry as "the second phase of True Parents' course, centering on True Mother."[160]

[155] H. J. H. Moon, "Let Us Inherit the Realm of True Parents' Victory and Begin a Future Filled with Hope," September 17, 2012, in *Forgive, Love, Unite: A Collection of True Mother's Words to Members since True Father's Ascension to the Spirit World, September 2012–December 2014* (Seoul: FFWPU International Headquarters, 2015), 69.

[156] H. J. H. Moon, "Being with True Father before and after His Ascension. Message sent to Regional headquarters and Mission Nations, September 23, 2012," in *Forgive, Love, Unite*, 33–34.

[157] H. J. H. Moon, "World Peace and the Role of Women," in *True Mother Hak Ja Han Moon: An Anthology, Book 2*, ed. Sunhak Institute of History (Seoul: Sung Hwa Publishing, 2018), 70.

[158] H. J. H. Moon, "Father's Words and Achievement Are Like a Gemstone" (January 9, 2013), www.tparents.org/Moon-Talks/HakJaHanMoon-13/HakJaHan-130109.htm, accessed March 9, 2022.

[159] H. J. H. Moon, "Special Assembly on Chuseok" [Korean Thanksgiving] (September 30, 2012), http://tparents.org/Moon-Talks/HakJaHanMoon/HakJaHan-120930.htm, accessed October 11, 2022.

[160] H. J. H. Moon, "True Mother's Address to the American Leaders" (October 1, 2012), www.tparents.org/Moon-Talks/HakJaHanMoon/HakJaHan-121001.pdf, accessed March 9, 2022.

Hak Ja Han's criticism of the way things had been done previously and her actions in redirecting UCM resources struck a discordant note. However, her really egregious violations – according to her critics – were changes she made to church traditions considered sacrosanct and untouchable as they had been established by Moon. Some actions were mostly symbolic. For example, she replaced the *Cheon Il Guk* national anthem Moon had selected with a more cheerful song and altered several phrases of Family Pledge, a staple of Unification devotion; this gave great offense, despite the fact that Moon had modified it several times previously. Other changes were more substantive. Less than a year after Moon's passing, she oversaw the publication of a revised version of the *Cheong Seong Gyeong* (Heavenly Scripture). She described her husband's sermons and speeches as "precious words" which, nonetheless, needed to be "polished" and put in order.[161]

A final trajectory of Mrs. Moon's leadership was her interpretation of core Unification doctrines from a gender-balanced perspective. In January 2013, Mrs. Moon directed that members address God not as "Heavenly Father," but as "Heavenly Parent."[162] She claimed that earlier ways of addressing God, such as Yahweh during the Old Testament period, or Heavenly Father during the New Testament period, were now superseded. Her doctrine of God flowed directly into her doctrine of Christ. Moon had stated that the mission of the Messiah was "a mission of True Parents."[163] However, many followers understood that Mrs. Moon's authority was wholly derivative and entirely dependent upon loyalty and obedience to her husband. This was a position that she explicitly rejected. After Moon's death, especially, she maintained a position of Christological equivalence. This was evident in her assertion of a unique and independent identity as God's "Only-Begotten Daughter."[164] As she put it, "God's only begotten son and God's only begotten daughter are equal. You cannot say that God's only begotten son educated God's only begotten daughter."[165] Essentially, Mrs. Moon was carving out an independent sphere of charismatic authority.

For three years after Moon's passing, Hak Ja Han Moon concentrated her efforts on internal UCM affairs, establishing her identity, focusing on grassroots evangelism and youth, and opening the UCM's Cheongpyeong Lake complex

---

[161] H. J. H. Moon, "True Mother with Members: New Year Celebration" (January 7, 2013), in *Forgive, Love, Unite*, 94.

[162] Ibid., 95.

[163] S. M. Moon, "True Parents and the Messiah," in *Cheon Seong Gyeong* [Heavenly Scripture] (Seoul: FFWPU, 2014), Book 2, Chapter 2, 163–83.

[164] Mickler, "Gender Politics in the Post-Sun Myung Moon Unification Movement," 211.

[165] H. J. H. Moon, "We Are One in Attending True Parents" (October 27, 2014), in *Forgive, Love, Unite*, 337.

as its international headquarters and model community. In 2015, a Korean magazine contrasted her efforts with that of "her husband who focused strongly on interreligious and peace movements."[166] However, that year, she launched a new public phase of her ministry that bore a striking resemblance to that of her late husband, including multiple peace initiatives, world summit gatherings, rallies in iconic arenas and stadiums, and international marriage Blessings. Evangelism was still a priority, but public events were meant to create an environment for witnessing. Earlier, in 2013, Mrs. Moon had utilized a strategy used by her late husband, establishing a seven-year mobilization timetable referred to as Vision 2020. She set the goal that by 2020, seven nations would be models of national restoration, meaning that they would have cohosted a UCM summit conference, a Blessing ceremony, which included national leadership – preferably the head of state, and a youth festival. Vision 2020 provided direction and focus, and was the driving force for FFWPU initiatives during the remainder of the decade.

Mrs. Moon began the public phase of her ministry in 2015. On the occasion of the third anniversary of Moon's death, having concluded a traditional Korean three-year period of mourning, she presided over the first Sunhak Peace Prize Awards Ceremony. Combining her own name with that of her late husband's first name ("Sun" and "Hak"), it was a Unification version of the Nobel Peace Prize. Thereafter, the prize was awarded biannually under designated themes to two recipients, each of whom received US$500,000. In 2016, she launched the International Association of Parliamentarians for Peace (IAPP) at the National Assembly of the Republic of Korea. For the remainder of that year, under the auspices of the UPF, the FFWPU inaugurated regional chapters in Nepal, Burkina Faso, England, Costa Rica, Paraguay, Zambia, and Japan. The capstone launch, convened in the Kennedy Caucus Room of the US Senate, concluded the series. Mrs. Moon commented, "I ha[ve] traveled the globe, going to six continents to convene these events," and claimed, "More than 20,000 people, including 2,500 incumbent parliamentarians from 190 nations … attended, making this initiative a great success."[167]

In 2017, Mrs. Moon moved beyond events by invitation in controlled settings by holding two high-risk, high-reward public rallies. Both were strikingly reminiscent of her husband's efforts to fill famous arenas and stadiums. The first was a "Peace Starts with Me" rally at New York City's Madison Square

---

[166] S. Sakuwa, trans., "Family Federation's Loving Care and Investment: The Best Chance to Visit North Korea," *Weekly Chosun* (May 25–31, 2015), www.tparents.org/Moon-Talks/HakJa HanMoon-15/HakJaHan-150525a.pdf, accessed October 11, 2022.

[167] H. J. H. Moon, *Mother of Peace: A Memoir* (Washington, DC: Washington Times Global Media Group, 2020), 311.

Garden in July. The second was a "Global Rally for the Peaceful Reunification of the Korean Peninsula" at Seoul's 80,000-seat capacity Sangam World Cup Stadium in November. The FFWPU mobilized its personnel and resources to fill both venues. The events particularly impacted developing nation contacts who were invited as guests. These successes inspired confidence in Hak Ja Han Moon's peace program and added to her credibility as a leader. The FFWPU began referring to her, and she began referring to herself, as the "Mother of Peace." In early 2018, Mrs. Moon traveled to Dakar, Senegal for a UCM-sponsored African Summit hosted by the Senegalese president with some 1,200 participants representing 60 countries.

Hak Ja Han Moon described her global ministry as a "cosmic march to Canaan" with the stated purpose of consecrating seven nations as models of national restoration. As noted, this meant that they would have cohosted a UCM summit conference, a Blessing ceremony, which included national leadership, and a youth festival. The first to do so was Sao Tome and Principe, a tiny equatorial island nation in the Gulf of Guinea, off the coast of Central Africa, in September 2019. Mrs. Moon declared the nation had become "Heavenly" Sao Tome and Principe.[168] By the end of the year, she had also consecrated heavenly Albania, Cambodia, Taiwan, Niger, Palau, and the Dominican Republic – seven nations in all. She also conducted a "continental" Blessing ceremony at South Africa's FNB Stadium in Johannesburg "with the heart of blessing a reborn continent, 'Heavenly Africa'."[169] These were largely symbolic victories. Nevertheless, having met her goal, she committed herself to the realization of a "Heavenly Unified Korea" and another seven-year course with the goal of a substantial portion of the world's people becoming citizens of *Cheon Il Guk* by 2027.

Amid COVID-19, Mrs. Moon convened "Rallies of Hope" beamed from a giant jumbotron from the UCM's World Peace Center at Cheonpyeong Lake, Korea. Intended to reach a mass audience, these included videotaped addresses from major leaders. The first rally, convened on August 8, 2020, featured keynote speeches by former UN Secretary General Ban Ki-moon, former US Speaker of the House Newt Gingrich, and Cambodian Prime Minister Hun Sen among others. The FFWPU claimed more than 2 million registered online viewers worldwide.[170] A second Rally of Hope in September featured addresses by former US Vice Presidents Dick Cheney and Dan Quayle and former Nigerian President Goodluck Jonathan. A sixth Rally of Hope, on May 8,

---

[168] H. J. H. Moon, *Mother of Peace*, 320. [169] Ibid., 342.

[170] Y. Yoon, "True Mother, the Mother of Peace Won a Great Victory at the Rally of Hope" (August 16, 2020), www.tparents.org/Moon-Talks/HakJaHan-20/HakJaHan-200816.pdf, accessed March 13, 2022.

2021, included addresses by former Trump-era officials, Vice President Mike Pence, Secretary of State Mike Pompeo and Secretary of Defense Mark Esper. A seventh Rally of Hope, on September 11, 2021, included former US President Donald Trump and former Japanese Prime Minister Shinzo Abe, both of whom delivered videotaped addresses.[171] Abe was assassinated on July 8, 2022 by Tetsuya Yamagami, aged forty-one, who reportedly held a grudge against the UCM for his mother's large monetary donations more than twenty years previously. He allegedly targeted Abe because of the former prime minister's perceived support of the movement. The tragic incident further strained relations between the UCM and broad sectors of the Japanese public.

The Rallies of Hope and associated organizations and events were long on symbolism and bore an unmistakable tilt to the right. This was somewhat balanced by centrist leaders such as Ban Ki-moon and representatives from the developing world. In addition, Mrs. Moon emphasized environmental degradation, ethnic and race relations, poverty and inequality, and questioned American gun culture. There was, perhaps, an unwieldy amount of ideological diversity in the coalition she fashioned. Nevertheless, she carved out a serviceable public persona as the Mother of Peace. In the course of a decade, she had pulled the FFWPU past the crisis of Moon's passing, withstood internal criticism, and developed a global ministry. However, the FFWPU's long-term future was still uncertain and internal opposition to Mrs. Moon's leadership coalesced around two of her sons and their breakaway groups.

5 Schismatic Organizations

The UCM, like other NRMs, endured high member turnover rates. However, there were few break-off groups of consequence, at least during Moon's lifetime. That changed after his death when two of his sons led schismatic organizations that siphoned off UCM resources and membership. Early splinter groups were charismatically led, in most cases short-lived, and animated by claims of Moon's failure or by depictions of him as a forerunner to their leader and group. After Moon's passing, Hyun Jin (Preston) Moon and Hyung Jin (Sean) Moon, respectively his eldest and youngest living sons, introduced a new dynamic, claiming to be his rightful successor. Both definitively broke from the FFWPU, sought to discredit and displace their mother, Hak Ja Han Moon, as leader of the UCM, and opposed each other.

---

[171] M. Papenfuss, "Trump Hails 'Moonie' Church Founders In Virtual 9/11 'Rally'," *Huffington Post* (September 13, 2021), www.huffpost.com/entry/trump-moonies-unification-church-hak-ja-han-moon-christofascist_n_613ec306e4b0640100a6884c, accessed April 3, 2022.

Splinter Groups

A few early splinter groups should be noted. One split occurred following the death of Moon and his wife's second son, Heung Jin, in a 1983 automobile accident. Afterwards, a number of spiritually inclined members in a variety of locations throughout the world professed to have channeled messages and received direct guidance from him. This culminated in a young Zimbabwean claiming to be Heung Jin Moon's embodiment. His claim gained credence, and Cleophas Kundiona ("Black Heung-Jin," as he was known) led a series of revival meetings attended by thousands of UC adherents worldwide in 1987–8.[172] After Kundiona exhibited violent behavior, Moon directed him to return to Africa, an order he did not follow. At this point, there was a consensus that Heung Jin's spirit had left Kundiona and an evil spirit had taken over. He turned on the UC, conducted a book burning of *Divine Principle*, and started a short-lived sect, drawing out a small number of southern Africa church members.

The Woo Group was a splinter group of longer duration. In 1993, the Korean UC excommunicated its leader, Woo Myung-Shik. Woo had joined the UC in 1974 and was blessed along with 6,000 couples in 1982. Afterwards, he asserted that original sin could not be liquidated through the Marriage Blessing of Moon and his wife but rather though sexual relations with himself. He encouraged his followers to infiltrate the UCM. Five Japanese UC members who aggressively recruited for the Woo Group were excommunicated in 1994. One of them, Okamoto Tatsunori, produced several works, including *95 Theses*, intended to reform the UCM, and *Principle of the Completed Testament Age* (2002). In 2000, Okamoto applied to be reinstated in the UC, having rejected the sexual excesses of the Woo Group. He was accepted but excommunicated again a year later. Japanese UC headquarters stated that it "considers anybody who consciously or unconsciously belongs to Mr. Okamoto's group . . . to be an extension of the Woo Group."[173] The Okamoto group made some headway in the Czech Republic, converting the church's former national leader.[174]

The Nakayama Group is a UC derivative whose leader eventually declared herself a living deity and pursued outreach beyond the UCM. In 2001–2, the Japanese UC headquarters issued letters warning its membership about a Nakayama–Shirabe Group or "Cosmic Federation of True Parents in Japan." Nakayama Yoshiko and her niece Shirabe Hiromi claimed that Unification teachings were the words of the masculine God which needed to be completed

---

[172] J. Beverley, "Spirit Revelation and the Unification Church," in *Controversial New Religions*, ed. J. Lewis and J. Petersen (New York: Oxford University Press, 2005), 47–49.

[173] T. Hashimoto, "The Teachings of Mr. Okamoto" (January 24, 2004), www.tparents.org/Library/Unification/Topics/Heresies/Hashimoto-040124a.htm, accessed December 9, 2021.

[174] Ibid.

by the words of the feminine God. They and their followers sent newsletters and distributed leaflets inviting church members to their gatherings. They gained an unknown but substantial number of ex-UC members. In 2006, Nakayama established a presence in the Philippines, took the name "Senyu Ryuka Sama" and, in 2010, claimed to be divine. In 2013, her group staged a coronation of the "Sun God Senyu Ryuka Sama" before a capacity crowd of 12,000 at the Cuneta Astrodome in the Philippines. Billed as "The Great Cosmic Advent Festival of Resurrection for the Opening of a New Age," it included an impressive array of dancers, lasers, and pyrotechnics accompanying Senyu Ryuka's entrance down a grand stairway and her elevation with crown and scepter on a pedestal, with more pyrotechnics.[175] Nakayama subsequently circulated her teachings or "Cosmic Tenets" on the Internet.

A Substantial Word group (c. 2015), similar to Nakayama, is headed by a female leader, KOMABA Kumiko, and originated in Japan. Like the Nakayama group, it puts special emphasis on the feminine, specifically Japanese women, who are understood to be vehicles of the Holy Spirit. However, to date, the group lacks the flamboyant qualities of Nakayama and is relatively secretive, limiting outreach to one-on-one witnessing, almost exclusively to FFWPU members. As its name suggests, it focuses on doctrine. In 2018, it published a 411-page volume, *Foundation Day and Seonghwa: The Kingdom of God Father Left Behind*, which details the ways the FFWPU misinterpreted and misapplied Moon's core teachings.[176] Substantial Word has followers in Japan, Brazil, Canada, and the United States and a presence in up to twenty-five other countries. In 2019, FFWPU Japan issued a warning about the "Komaba Group," stating that its adherents "pretend to be church members" and "plant doubts in people's faith."[177]

Providence Church, officially the Christian Gospel Mission, also known as Jesus Morningstar (JMS), is the most controversial organization linked to the UCM. It does not function as a UCM splinter group because it does not acknowledge a connection to it and does not seek to siphon off UCM members. Its founder, JUNG Myung-seok (b. 1945), was a member of the UC during the 1970s but in 1980 he founded the Ae-chun church, affiliated with the Methodist Church. Expelled due to Jung's messianic claims, the group changed its name to the International Christian Association and, in 1999, the Christian Gospel

---

[175] 'Master Blaster,' "Searching for Senyu Ryuka, the Japanese woman people call 'God'," *Sora News* 24 (November 12, 2013), https://soranews24.com/2013/11/12/searching-for-senyu-ryuka-the-japanese-woman-people-call-god/, accessed December 9, 2021.

[176] Substantial Word Research Group, *Foundation Day and Seonghwa: The Kingdom of God Father Left Behind* (Aletheia Naos, 2018).

[177] "Komaba Group Info," *How Well Do You Know Your Moon?* [blog], https://howwelldoyouknowyourmoon.tumblr.com/search/Komaba, accessed December 11, 2021.

Mission. Critics allege affinities between Jung's *Thirty Lessons* and Unification teachings.[178] Providence established *Wolmyeongdong*, a retreat center that resembles the UCM's Cheonpyeong Lake complex, and conducted group weddings, though not on the scale of the UCM. With branches in Japan, Australia, Taiwan, and Hong Kong, members are recruited through activity circles, such as sport, music, or modelling clubs. Providence Church, like the Woo Group, included teachings that original sin could be liquidated through sexual relations with the founder. Jung was convicted of rape by a Korean court in 2008 and served ten years in prison.

Splinter groups were an irritant but not a threat to the UCM. That changed after Moon's death and schismatic organizations led by Moon's eldest and youngest living sons became a more serious problem. The eldest, Hyun Jin (Preston, or "H1" in FFWPU parlance) broke from the FFWPU in 2009, refused to give up major UCM assets he controlled in Korea and the Americas, and eventually set up the Family Peace Association as an alternative to the FFWPU. The youngest, Hyung Jin (Sean, or "H2" in FFWPU parlance), broke away from the FFWPU over a two-year period (2013–15), continued using the UC logo for his services, and set up the World Peace and Unification Sanctuary (Sanctuary Church) in Newfoundland, Pennsylvania as an alternative to the FFWPU. The brothers' actions did not deter the FFWPU from its public ministry but were an unwelcome intrusion.

Organizations Led by Hyun Jin (Preston) Moon

Hyun Jin Moon was the first of the two brothers to take a leadership role in the FFWPU. A graduate of Columbia University (BA History, 1995) and Harvard Business School (MBA, 1998), he was appointed international vice president of the FFWPU in 1998. An energetic speaker with a revivalist style, he committed himself to the education of the movement's second generation. In 2000, he was appointed international president of World CARP, the church's collegiate association, and in 2001, head of the Youth Federation for World Peace, a church affiliate. He led the FFWPU's Special Task Force, a two-year missionary program for high school graduates, and founded Service for Peace, an international service and educational NGO. In 2006, Hyun Jin became chairman of the Unification Church International (UCI). This was a significant appointment that went beyond education or youth ministry. The UCI controlled major UCM assets in the United States, including *The Washington Times* and its parent company, News World Communications, of which he became chairman. The UCI also controlled the UCM's highly valued Yeoido Island property in the

---

[178] M. Tahk, 기독교 이단 연구 [Study on Christian Cults] (1986).

heart of Seoul's financial district and the JW Marriott Central City hotel/mall complex in Seoul's major transportation hub. In 2007, Hyun Jin became cochair of the UPF, which coordinated FFWPU's nonprofits. This was the concluding appointment in his portfolio and the platform from which he attempted to remake the church.[179]

Despite his rapid ascent through the FFWPU hierarchy, Hyun Jin was avowedly anti-theological and anti-institutional. He was a strong advocate of Moon's teachings as a revelation from God, but impatient with theological debate and convinced that his father had not come to establish a church.[180] Hyun Jin mobilized UPF and FFWPU memberships to support a series of Global Peace Festivals (GPFs) in 2008. These were large-scale, multiday events that included conferences of VIPs, many of whom were flown in and feted in hotels. GPF activities included service projects, greetings from local dignitaries, a keynote address delivered by Hyun Jin, and festivals held in public venues, often stadiums in smaller countries, that featured local headliner entertainment. The UPF and the FFWPU sponsored GPFs in cities around the world – from Asunción, Paraguay and Nairobi, Kenya to Ulaanbaatar, Mongolia and Kuala Lumpur, Malaysia. Other locales included capital cities such as Brasilia, Washington, DC, Ottawa, Haifa, Tokyo, Seoul, and Manila. Hyun Jin claimed the festivals would position the UCM as a "global peace movement" and bring the culture of the FFWPU's International Marriage Blessing "into the main-stream on the worldwide level."[181]

The reaction of FFWPU members to GPFs was mixed. Many were impressed and agreed with Hyun Jin that his father had not come to establish another church or denomination. At the same time, there was resistance. It was one thing to be mobilized by Moon senior but, as one church scholar noted, "It is . . . very difficult for hereditary charisma to demand the same or stronger dedication from the original founder's followers."[182] In addition, the GPFs were expensive and remuneration was elusive. Hyun Jin had a coterie of devoted followers but a penchant for launching initiatives without official authorization and reported to Moon in ways that did not fully acknowledge his father's spiritual authority. In a 2008 "Report to Parents," he claimed to be "leading the movement in a clear methodical manner, aligned to the providence of God" and called for all major FFWPU nonprofits to "subordinate and align their activities and initiatives" with "the global goals and aims of UPF," which he led. He also called for the

---

179 Mickler, "The Post-Sun Myung Moon Unification Church," 48.   180 Ibid., 48–49.
181 H. J. (Preston) Moon, "Activities and Future Directions," *Today's World* 28, no. 8 (2007): 11.
182 Y. Masuda, "Moral Vision and Practice in the Unification Movement," unpublished Ph.D. dissertation, University of Southern California, 1987, 386–87.

creation, under his direction, of "a global economic engine . . . with the explicit purpose of financially supporting UPF."[183]

Less than a month later, Moon appointed Hyun Jin's youngest brother, Hyung Jin, international president of the FFWPU, clearly bypassing Hyun Jin. Moon then appointed Hyung Jin president of World CARP and the Youth Federation for World Peace, organizations which Hyun Jin had previously led. This turn of events was a shocking reversal, especially for Hyun Jin. Many within the UCM regarded him as the presumptive successor to Moon and he had been conducting himself as the putative heir. In early 2009, Hyun Jin attempted unsuccessfully to wrest control of the HSA-UWC US Board of Directors from his sister, In Jin (Tatiana) Moon, who, he alleged, had been appointed chair due to the machinations of his younger brothers. This resulted in Moon asking him to cease all public activities and live with him for a year, a request Hyun Jin rejected. Both sides sought to avoid a split, but mediation efforts and a face-to-face meeting were unsuccessful. In November 2009, Moon removed Hyun Jin as chair of the UPF and appointed Hyung Jin, which prompted a definitive break. In a letter to the UPF's Presiding Council, Hyun Jin wrote that he "will devote my heart and soul to developing the Global Peace Festival series" but that they "will not go forward as projects of UPF, and will have no formal or legal association with FFWPU." He pronounced himself "committed as ever to UPF's original ideals and to my Father's peace messages," but he had clearly moved beyond the bounds of his father's authority.[184]

These pronouncements resulted in turmoil. Those loyal to, or in the employ of, Hyun Jin continued their association. Others were confused. The FFWPU's international headquarters directed that members and UCM organizations should not take part or be involved in Hyun Jin's activities.[185] In the immediate aftermath of Hyun Jin's departure, conflict over GPFs spilled over into the wider UCM. In the Philippines, Hyun Jin's followers used their connections to have the FFWPU's South Asian regional director deported. In Nepal, the FFWPU succeeded in having the Nepalese president and prime minister withdraw from GPFs' main event. In Mongolia, division between the Global Peace Festival Foundation (GPFF) and the FFWPU resulted in an open schism. Members of a new Mongolian Peoples' Federation for World Peace locked the FFWPU

[183] H .J. (Preston) Moon, "Report to Parents" (March 23, 2008), www.tparents.org/Moon-Talks/HyunJinMoon/HyunJinMoon-080323.htm, accessed December 9, 2021.

[184] H. J. (Preston) Moon, "Letter from the Co-Chair of the UPF Presiding Council" (November 4, 2009), www.tparents.org/Moon-Talks/HyunJinMoon/HyunJinMoon-091104.htm, accessed December 9, 2021.

[185] H. J. (Sean) Moon, "Establishing and Engaging in Activities of GPF (or GPFF, GPC, GPA)." FFWPU International Headquarters Memo (March 24, 2010), www.tparents.org/Moon-Talks/HyungJinMoon-10/HyungJinMoon-100324.htm, accessed December 9, 2021.

headquarters building, smashed the car windshield of Moon's longtime personal assistant, and circulated a resolution attacking the FFWPU. In 2010, Hyun Jin and his supporters commandeered the pulpit of the Brazilian headquarters church in São Paulo, bodily removing the FFWPU continental director in a chaotic scene during a national service. Videos of this and of Hyun Jin berating and alternately kicking and slapping the Brazilian national leader went viral within the UCM, precipitating an uproar. This resulted in Moon issuing a handwritten declaration affirming his support for the FFWPU World Mission department and Hyung Jin (Sean) Moon as its representative. He warned that others who claim such a position are "the heretic and the destroyer."[186]

Hyun Jin persisted with his leadership claims but had no realistic prospect of asserting authority within the FFWPU. What power he did possess was over the Unification Church International (UCI), a nonprofit, charitable corporation set up in the District of Columbia, United States in 1977 to support UC activities worldwide. As relations deteriorated with his younger brothers, and eventually his parents, Hyun Jin took action to solidify his control of UCI. He succeeded in having two business associates elected directors at a UCI board meeting in 2009 and obtained the resignations of two directors placed on the board previously at the recommendation of Moon. That gave him majority control of the five-member board. He and his two board allies subsequently voted the remaining two directors recommended by Moon off the UCI board, adding Hyun Jin's brother in-law and another close associate and making his takeover of UCI complete.

Control of UCI was a double-edged sword. On the one hand, it gave Hyun Jin control of major UCM assets in the United States and Korea. On the other hand, a number of them had high maintenance costs or were dependent on financial subsidies from the FFWPU, primarily from Japan. A prominent example was *The Washington Times*, the UCM's flagship media enterprise. From 2006–9, UCI benefited from UCJ subsidies to *The Washington Times*, totaling upwards of US$35 million a year.[187] Now that Hyun Jin effected what the FFWPU regarded as a hostile takeover, that funding ceased. In 2010, UCI sold *The Washington Times* and its debt to TWT Holdings, a company owned by HSA-UWC, for US $1.[188] The UCI board also amended its Articles of Incorporation, changing the corporate name from "Unification Church International" to simply UCI and deleting all references to supporting Unification Churches worldwide. That year, UCI began selling off UCM assets, ostensibly to support GPFs and

[186] S. M. Moon, "June 5th Declaration" (June 5, 2010), www.tparents.org/Moon-Talks/SunMyung Moon10/SunMyungMoon-100605.htm, accessed March 8, 2022.

[187] I. Shapira, "Church Plans to Sell *Washington Times*," *Washington Post* (May 1, 2010): A11.

[188] I. Shapira, "Moon Group Buys Back *Washington Times*," *Washington Post* (November 3, 2010): C1.

other activities. Sales included an office building in Washington, DC near the US Capitol for US$113 million and the 417-room Sheraton National Hotel in Arlington, Virginia, a venue for FFWPU events, for an undisclosed sum. Assets including UCI's stake in Seoul's Central City Marriott Hotel and shopping complex, the Parc1 Yeoido development, Yong Pyong Ski resort, and Il Sung construction corporation were donated to a newly created Kingdom Investment Foundation, an organization with no connection to the FFWPU.

These actions resulted in lawsuits and unwanted publicity. The Korean UC sued to block the construction of a 72- and a 56-story skyscraper under the auspices of UCI on its Yeoido Island property, a project with a projected cost of US$2.1 billion. The Family Federation for World Peace and Unification International (FFWPUI), UPF, UCJ, and two ousted UCI directors filed suit against Hyun Jin Moon and UCI board members in the Superior Court of the District of Columbia, United States, alleging usurpation of UCI and its assets. A South Korean media outlet described developments as the "Battle of the Princes" within the UC.[189] In the United States, a maze of motions and counter-motions, a fight over tainted evidence, and clashes over continued dissipation and transfer of assets tied up the UCI case in court for seven years. In 2018, the trial judge issued a summary judgment in favor of the FFWPUI. In 2020, the court ordered that Preston Moon and three defendants be removed as directors of UCI and held liable to UCI for a surcharge in the amount of US$532 million, along with prejudgment interest.[190] On August 25, 2022, the DC Court of Appeals reversed the order for summary judgment, which FFWPUI has appealed.

Amid these struggles, Hyun Jin continued work under the auspices of the Global Peace Foundation, though at a lesser pace than previously. In 2012, he founded Action for Korea United, a coalition of Korean civic groups working for reunification, and in 2014 published *Korea Dream: A Vision for a Unified Korea*. The Global Peace Foundation launched a One Korea Global Campaign which sponsored annual peace conventions and cultural initiatives. In 2017, Hyun Jin formally inaugurated the Family Peace Association (FPA). Stating he could "no longer work through FFWPU," he dedicated it as the "new vehicle" to realize his father's vision.[191] For all of his insistence that Moon had not come to

---

[189] S. Kwon, "In-Depth Report Legal Dispute over the Unification Church-Owned Parking Lot in Yeouido, Seoul" [unofficial translation], *Chosun Monthly* (January 23, 2011), www.tparents .org/Moon-Talks/KookJinMoon/KookJinMoon-110123.pdf, accessed December 11, 2021.

[190] J. Anderson, "Order Granting, in Part, Plaintiffs' Motion for Remedies for the Individual Defendants' Breach of Fiduciary Duty," Superior Court of the District of Columbia – Civil Division, 2011 CA 003721 B (December 3, 2020).

[191] H. J. (Preston) Moon, "Family Peace Association Inaugural Ceremony Founder's Address" (December 2, 2017), https://family-peace.org/2017/12/hyun-jin-moon/family-peace-associ ation-inaugural-ceremony-founders-address/, accessed December 11, 2021.

start a religion, the FPA came dangerously close to being one. A leading scholar of new religions has noted, "Despite FPA representatives arguing that it is not a religion, the organization has all the trappings of one: a set of holy scriptures ... observance of holy days, a type of pledge that is recited, Sunday school for children, communal reading of holy texts, spiritual retreats, [a] marriage blessing ceremony (from 2015), and other rituals."[192] In founding the Global Peace Foundation and the Family Peace Association, Hyun Jin set up organizations that mirrored the UPF and the FFWPU, only with himself as the head.

Organizations Led by Hyung Jin (Sean) Moon

Hyung Jin (Sean) Moon assumed a leadership role within the FFWPU later than Hyun Jin, but his rise was even more rapid.[193] He was a graduate of Harvard Extension School (ALB Liberal Arts, 2004) and Harvard Divinity School (MA Comparative Religion, 2006). He experienced a religious awakening following the death of an older brother in 1999, shaved his head, donned Buddhist clothing, and began an intense regimen of meditation and spiritual practices. He published *A Bald Head and a Strawberry* (2005), an account of his spiritual journey, and *Cheon-Hwa-Dang: The House of Heaven's Harmony* (2006), an effort to reconcile religious asceticism and family life. During this period, Hyung Jin began to attend his father in the manner of a devotee and "to develop a scholarly interest in Unificationism."[194] After completing his studies he moved to Korea, intent on being a religious practitioner rather than an academic. Within six months, he went from being the minister of a small congregation in the Western Seoul region to senior pastor of the Seoul headquarters church. He reportedly conducted six services a week and increased congregational attendance tenfold[195] In 2008, Moon appointed him rather than his elder brother Hyun Jin international president of the FFWPU. Hyung Jin later displaced Hyun Jin as president of World CARP, chair of the Youth Federation for Word Peace, and chair of the UPF, which precipitated Hyun Jin's initial break from the FFWPU.

Hyung Jin made it clear he intended to steer the FFWPU in an explicitly religious direction. On becoming international president, he repudiated the peace movement orientation of Hyun Jin, stating, "I studied religion for seven years ...

[192] M. Introvigne, "Preston Moon and the Family Peace Association." Presentation at CESNUR Conference (2016), Daejin University, Korea, www.cesnur.org/2016/mi_preston_moon.pdf, accessed December 11, 2021.

[193] Mickler, "The Post-Sun Myung Moon Unification Church," 52.

[194] H. J. (Sean) Moon, *A Bald Head and a Strawberry* (Tarrytown, NY: Sincerity Publications, 2005), 11

[195] J. Seuk, "Bridges Connecting Everyone to True Parents," www.tparents.org/Library/Unification/Talks2/Seuk/Seuk-080820.htm, accessed March 13, 2022.

No matter how much we say we are not a religion ... we are most definitely a religion."[196] Some were wary of Hyung Jn's spiritual practices. Early on, his *jeongseong* (devotional) conditions in support of movement efforts included 12,000 bows over a 6-day period and writing out the Chinese character for "sincerity" (*seong*) in his own blood. Others were taken aback by his doctrinal interpretations. His elder brother Hyun Jin understood Moon to be the Lord of the Second Advent but regarded efforts to deify him as absurd. Hyung Jin affirmed a qualitative difference between his parents – who, like Christ, derived from the seed or essence (Logos) of God – and the rest of humanity.[197] However, many appreciated his sense of religious vocation, associated his asceticism with accounts of Moon's early life, and welcomed his approachability. In the end, it was Moon's view that mattered. Not only did he appoint Hyung Jin international president of FFWPU, but he also stated that Hyung Jin and his wife "will become the pillars of our house in the future."[198] Hyung Jin claimed not just to have been appointed but anointed. In two ceremonies presided over by Moon, Hyung Jin and his wife marched attired in the same royal garb and crowns that his parents had worn on previous occasions.

The challenge for Hyung Jin was Moon's death on September 3, 2012. As noted, Hak Ja Han Moon acted decisively to consolidate her position as head of the FFWPU. This included reassigning Hyung Jin to the United States. He was sent to replace his sister In Jin (Tatiana) Moon who either resigned or was fired by Mrs. Moon as head of FFWPU USA when it became known that she had carried on an extramarital affair and secretly born a child. Although he retained his position as president of FFWPU International and FFWPU Korea, Hyung Jin's leadership of them effectively ceased. In October, due to disagreements over UCM finances, Mrs. Moon called for the resignation of Kook Jin (Justin) Moon, another of Hyung Jin's elder brothers, as chair of the Tongil Foundation, which controlled UCM businesses in Korea. Hyung Jin considered Kook Jin an organizational genius and relied on his support. Still, Hyung Jin accepted these directives. In doing so, he conceded that Mrs. Moon's status as UCM cofounder superseded his as heir apparent. However, when Mrs. Moon directed that he step down as head of FFWPU USA and return to Korea, he resisted. In a public letter, he wrote,

> As you know True Mother announced that we will be let go from our role as president of HSA-UWC America. My wife and I were a little surprised as this is the third time that we have been "let go of" since Father's ascension with no prior guidance or explanation given for termination. It would be dishonest to

[196] H. J. (Sean) Moon, "Inaugural Address," *Today's World* 29, no. 3 (April 2008): 23.
[197] H. J. (Sean) Moon, "The Messianic Identity," *Today's World* 33, no. 1 (January 2012): 1, 13–17.
[198] S. M. Moon, "Become an Inheritor," *Today's World* 29 no. 4 (May 2008): 4.

say that it does not hurt (again) or baffle us but we have always had a positive outlook on life and that won't change! We still move forward as the International President knowing God is good and that He is good all the time![199]

This was Hyung Jin's initial acknowledgment, at least publicly, that a rift had opened between him and his mother.

Having refused the direction of his mother to take up duties under her in Korea, Hyung Jin relocated to Newfoundland, Pennsylvania, where he began an independent ministry. He was joined by his elder brother, Kook Jin, who, though removed as head of the Tongil Foundation, owned Kahr Arms, a US small arms manufacturer. In 2013, Kook Jin announced plans to move the company to a new manufacturing facility in Pike County, Pennsylvania. Hyung Jin and Kook Jin purchased a Newfoundland church building in 2014 and began the World Peace and Unification Sanctuary, or Sanctuary Church. Initially, Hyung Jin elevated gifts of grace and the Holy Spirit. However, over time, his sermons turned apocalyptic. He castigated "predatory elites" and "postmodern" thinking, gave credence to "truther" claims about the Twin Tower attacks, and pushed end-time predictions.[200] In January 2015, he broke decisively with the FFWPU. His epiphany was that that the "predatory system of control ... in the world at large" also characterized the FFWPU.[201]

The situation was ambiguous and inflammatory since Hyung Jin was still technically FFWPU international president. In a January 2015 sermon titled "Breaking the Silence," he attacked the FFWPU's leadership. In February 2015, he announced the removal of all current leaders of the Unification Movement, declaring that they had "no authority."[202] He called on members to take over church boards and elect replacements. In March, the FFWPU removed Hyung Jin as international president, replacing him with Sun Jin (Selena) Moon, an older sister. This radicalized his position. Previously, he called for the liberation of his mother from a "dark alliance" of FFWPU clerics. He referred to the Stockholm Syndrome and claimed that Mrs. Moon identified with her captors.[203] After being removed from his position as international president, he attacked her directly. He declared her "authority and power" to be "stripped

---

[199] H. J. (Sean) Moon, "Letter to Unification Church USA" (February 24, 2013), http://tparents.org/Moon-Talks/HyungJinMoon-13/HyungJinMoon-130224.pdf, accessed December 11, 2021.

[200] M. Mickler, "The Sanctuary Church Schismatics," *Applied Unificationism* (December 14, 2015), https://appliedunificationism.com/2015/12/14/the-sanctuary-church-schism/, accessed December 11, 2021.

[201] Ibid.

[202] H. J. Moon, "Declaration of Heaven" (February 8, 2015), http://tparents.org/Moon-Talks/HyungJinMoon-13/HyungJinMoon-150215.pdf, accessed December 11, 2021.

[203] H. J. (Sean) Moon, "God Save the Queen" (January 25, 2015), http://tparents.org/Moon-Talks/HyungJinMoon-13/HyungJinMoon-150125.pdf, accessed December 11, 2021.

away and removed."[204] He announced her displacement as True Mother, referred to her thenceforth as the Han Mother (in reference to her maiden name), claimed she had been spiritually seduced, and denounced her as the "Whore of Babylon."[205] In 2017, he conducted a ceremony, divorcing Moon from the Han Mother and marrying him posthumously to the "perfection level True Mother," KANG Hyun Shil, a ninety-year old follower.

These were in-house developments and did not register with the wider public. But that changed dramatically in February 2018 when the Sanctuary Church held a Marriage Blessing/renewal ceremony at which participants wore crowns and carried AR-15 rifles. In his study of the Book of Revelation (2:27), Hyung Jin concluded that the reference to a rod of iron was "Bible-speak for the AR-15" and that Christ required armed kings and queens to defend his Kingdom.[206] He organized the Marriage Blessing ceremony to dramatize this. Approximately 500 followers from the United States and overseas took part, bearing AR-15s that were not loaded. Safety zip ties were employed and local and state police were invited to be on the site. The ceremony was highly controversial in itself, but because it was held two weeks after the Parkland, Florida shooting at Marjory Stoneman Douglas High School in which seventeen students were killed by a former student armed with the same weapon, it sparked national and international news coverage. This resulted in notoriety but also afforded a platform from which Hyung Jin extended his reach beyond the UCM.

He did so through Rod of Iron Ministries and a live, three-hour daily webcast, "The Kings Report," which defended the US constitution's Second Amendment and attacked gun control advocates. Hyung Jin frequently interviewed Second Amendment advocates, such as Gun Owners of America's Larry Pratt. In 2019, Rod of Iron Ministries sponsored a Freedom Festival on the 620-acre Kahr Arms property. In 2021, the festival included speeches by former National Rifle Association spokesperson Dana Loesch and former Trump strategist and senior counselor Steve Bannon.[207] Hundreds of firearms enthusiasts participated. Eric Trump spoke at Kahr Arms headquarters at its 2016 grand opening and during the 2020 presidential campaign. Hyung Jin was frequently pictured with a crown of bullets and a gold AR-15, both of which displayed variations of the UC logo.

---

[204] H. J. (Sean) Moon, "The King Reigns Forever" (March 15, 2015), www.tparents.org/Moon-Talks/HyungJinMoon-13/HyungJinMoon-150315a.pdf, accessed December 11, 2021.

[205] H. J. (Sean) Moon, "The Mystery of Babylon" (September 13, 2015), www.tparents.org/Moon-Talks/HyungJinMoon-13/HyungJinMoon-150913a.pdf, accessed December 11, 2021.

[206] T. Dunkel, "Locked and Loaded for the Lord," *Washington Post* (May 21, 2018): 6–20.

[207] Rod of Iron Freedom Festival, "2022 Speakers," www.rodofironfreedomfestival.org/speakers, accessed December 12, 2021.

This prompted the FFWPU to file a trademark infringement lawsuit. The FFWPU described Sanctuary Church's "gun-centered theology" as repugnant to its tenets and stated that news accounts of Sanctuary's gun wedding did little to differentiate it from the FFWPU, creating confusion in the public's mind. Its complaint noted that the UC symbol had been in use for more than fifty years and legally trademarked since 2009.[208] Sanctuary Church argued that the logo was a universal symbol at the core of Unification faith and could not be owned by anyone – any more than the Catholic Church could "obtain trademark registration for the cross" and prevent access to Lutherans and Methodists.[209] The FFWPU denied that the symbol identified a general class of spiritual organizations rather than a single, unique organization and cited court decisions against splinter groups "divorced from the charter of the primary Church" that seek to "adopt the Church's emblem."[210] On March 30, 2022, the trial court determined that it lacked jurisdiction over the matter because, in the court's estimation, it could not resolve the claims without entering into areas protected by First Amendment religion clauses. The court therefore declined to rule on the cross motions for summary judgment and dismissed the entire case for lack of subject matter jurisdiction.[211]

In a separate action, Hyung Jin filed a complaint against Hak Ja Han Moon, HSA-UWC, the FFWPU, and eight church officials in February 2019. His lawsuit alleged that Moon senior appointed him successor and leader of the Family Federation and UC in 2009 and that "Mrs. Moon and her co-conspirators orchestrated a malicious and illegal scheme to seize control of these organizations" and strip him of his proper authority. He brought the action "seeking a declaration of this Court to confirm his legal status as leader."[212] In December 2019, the Court dismissed the lawsuit in its entirety for lack of subject matter jurisdiction, stating that the US "First Amendment serves to prevent exactly this sort of picking winners in ecclesiastical matters."[213]

---

[208] *Holy Spirit Association for the Unification of World Christianity* v. *World Peace and Unification Sanctuary, Inc.*, Case No. 3:18-cv-01508-RDM (M.D.Pa) (July 30, 2018).

[209] "Defendants Brief," *Holy Spirit Association for the Unification of World Christianity* v. *World Peace and Unification Sanctuary, Inc.*, Case No. 3:18-cv-01508-RDM (M.D.Pa) (December 7, 2018).

[210] "Plaintiff's Reply Brief," *Holy Spirit Association for the Unification of World Christianity* v. *World Peace and Unification Sanctuary, Inc.*, Case No. 3:18-cv-01508-RDM (M.D.Pa) (December 28, 2018).

[211] J. Wilson, "Memorandum," *Holy Spirit Association for the Unification of World Christianity* v. *World Peace and Unification Sanctuary, Inc.*, Case No. 3:18-cv-01508-JPW (M.D.Pa) (March 30, 2022).

[212] *Hyung Jin "Sean" Moon* v. *Hak Ja Han Moon et al.*, No. 1:19-cv-01705-NRB (S.D.N.Y.) (February 22, 2019).

[213] N. Buchwald, "Memorandum and Order," Case No. 1:19-cv-017015-NRB (S.D.N.Y.) (December 29, 2019).

Hyung Jin filed an unsuccessful appeal to the US Court of Appeals for the Second District in March 2020 which was denied. In April 2021, he filed a petititon for certiori to the US Supreme Court, which was denied on June 14, 2021.

Hyung Jin Moon's conflict with the FFWPU, as that of his elder brother, Hyun Jin, was asymmetrical. Organizations led by the brothers possessed only a small fraction of the FFWPU's membership and resources. For the vast majority of those who had followed her husband, Hak Ja Han Moon has consolidated her position as FFWPU and UCM leader. However, she is a near-octogenarian and provisions for leadership going forward will be crucial. Additionally, the FFWPU will need to hold together its diverse membership base, including those born into the faith, lessen tensions with its host societies, and maintain transformative fervor in the face of pressures to accommodate and institutionalize. How the UCM manages its complex inner workings and external relations will determine its post–Sun Myung Moon/post–Hak Ja Han Moon fate.

6 Conclusions

Fredrick Sontag, a philosopher-theologian, published *Sun Myung Moon and the Unification Church* in 1977. Written at the height of the 1970s cult controversies, he was at pains to clarify how and why the book was written. He conducted dozens of interviews with UC members and opponents in Europe, the United States, Japan, and Korea as well as a six-hour question and answer session with Moon, which took up thirty pages in the book. At the end, Sontag stated, "I did come to two firm conclusions: (1) The origins of the movement are genuinely humble, religious, and spiritual (which many doubt); and (2) the adaptability and solidarity of the movement are such that we are dealing with a movement that is here to stay."[214] Although it was written nearly fifty years ago, Sontag's conclusions resonate with the UCM's historical record as documented in this account.

Moon's origins were clearly humble; he was born in the countryside in what is now North Korea to a family of rice farmers who sold off a major portion of their land during the occupation of the peninsula by imperial Japan (1905–45). To be sure, Moon rose above his circumstances, pursuing education beyond his local village school in Seoul and Tokyo. As an engineering graduate, he accepted employment with a Japanese-owned construction firm in Seoul prior to the end of the Second World War. At the same time, his early religious zeal and life-changing encounter with Christ in 1935 competed with any aspirations

---

[214] F. Sontag, Sun Myung *Moon and the Unification Church* (Nashville, TN: Abingdon, 1977), 12.

he may have had for a conventional life. He recalls that he received a sudden revelation in 1946 to cross over the 38th parallel and find the "people of God" in the North, leaving behind his first wife and newborn son. From there, he endured arrest and labor camp imprisonment. Freed by Allied bombardments, he lived as a refugee in the South, constructing a hillside hut out of mud, rock, and cardboard boxes.

What was true of Moon in the earliest phases of his life and ministry was also true of the UCM. It was born in a tiny ramshackle Seoul residence in 1954 and the movement was largely impoverished. During the 1950s, its only economic activities of note were the reselling canceled postage stamps and the sale of hand-tinted black-and-white photographs of famous places or popular entertainment personalities. The church in Japan likewise funded itself in the 1960s through *haihin kaishu*, the door-to-door collection of newspapers, magazines, bottles, and old clothing to be resold to junk dealers. In the 1970s, fledgling US and European missions funded themselves by selling flowers and candy. Members also followed Moon's religious course; their own life-changing encounters were mediated through his teachings and example. They also pursued single-minded religious vocations, enduring deprivation and often mockery and abuse, including involuntary confinement, while exiling themselves from families, careers, and conventional lives.

This narrative of origins is disputed by UCM opponents. Critics characterized the UCM as a political organization, a business masquerading as a religion, and claimed it originated as a 1950s sex cult. The UCM spent a great deal of time and resources combatting these claims. It was not able to fully reverse them, but by Moon's death in 2012 many of its public battles had subsided and the UCM entered a new phase. Rather than addressing an uncomprehending and often hostile external environment, the UCM's challenge was to maintain vibrancy and coherence in the face of internal pressures to either settle down into a form unrecognizable to its founders or split apart. Sontag concluded that the adaptability and solidarity of the movement were such that the UCM was here to stay. This second conclusion also resonates with the historical record.

The UCM was not a localized phenomenon. Despite being rooted in the Korean religious context, it evidenced a capacity to transcend its country of origin and adapt to multiple national settings, absorbing new traits from diverse host societies. In this it was distinct, even unique, among Korean NRMs. Very early on, the UCM spread to Japan where growth outstripped that in its homeland, and the UCM took on a more organized, corporate profile. The UCM then made a bigger leap, transplanting itself to the West. There, it gained greater sophistication in relating to societal elites and in coalition-building. The UCM exported these characteristics globally. Aside from geographical expansion, the UCM demonstrated ideological adaptability in adjusting to new historical circumstances. A prominent example was its post-Cold War shift from an anti-communist profile to a peace movement orientation. Following Moon's death, the UCM shifted from male to female leadership at the apex of the organization.

Despite its broad geographical spread and multinational membership base, the UCM maintained high levels of internal solidarity throughout its early history. This may be attributed to members' belief in the founders' exemplary character and charismatic leadership, the clarity of UCM core doctrines, and the UCM's standing as a high-demand group that winnowed out the less committed. Beyond that, the UCM facilitated affective bonds among its membership through common rituals, notably the Marriage Blessing, holy days, holy songs, communal worship, a liturgical calendar, local and international news-letters and magazines (both print and online), websites, and the emergence of a historiographical tradition that included cherished stories of steadfastness amid deprivation and suffering. In addition, the UCM encouraged large families (Mrs. Moon gave birth to fourteen children) and dedicated resources to youth education.

Sontag's conclusions regarding the UCM's staying power and their reson-ance with the record documented in this account are provisional. The UCM is less than seven decades old and its development could trend differently. American sociologist of religion Rodney Stark has referred to "the crisis of confidence that awaits most new religious movements as the founding gener-ation reaches the end of their lives."[215] According to him, "The record of new faiths suggests that unless the movement reaches a persuasive appearance of major success within the first generation, the founders will lose hope and turn the movement inward – adopt a new rhetoric that de-emphasizes growth and conversion."[216] That has not been the case up to this point. In fact, the UCM's founding generation has set its sights on significant global expansion. Sontag described UCM accomplishments until 1977 as "rather phenomenal."[217] Whether the post–Sun Myung Moon/post–Hak Ja Han Moon UCM will seek a denominational niche within which it might perpetuate, or whether it will maintain its world-transforming religious fervor, will be pivotal questions during the next stage of its development.

---

[215] R. Stark, "How New Religions Succeed: A Theoretical Model." In *The Future of New Religious Movements*, ed. R. Stark (Macon, GA: Mercer University Press, 1987), 21.

[216] Ibid.   [217] Sontag, *Sun Myung Moon and the Unification Church*, 12.

References

Anderson, J. "Order Granting, in Part, Plaintiffs' Motion for Remedies for the Individual Defendants' Breach of Fiduciary Duty." Superior Court of the District of Columbia – Civil Division, 2011 CA 003721 B, December 3, 2020.

Barker, E. *The Making of a Moonie: Choice or Brainwashing?* Oxford: Blackwell Publishing, 1984.

Baughman, J. "Massive Education." *Today's World* 13, no. 4 (April 1992): 20–25.

Beverley, J. "Spirit Revelation and the Unification Church." In *Controversial New Religions*, eds. J. Lewis and J. Petersen, 43–60. New York: Oxford University Press, 2005.

Blau, E. "Sun Myung Moon, Prophet to Thousands, Stirs Waves of Controversy As He Prepares for Big Rally Here." *New York Times* (September 16, 1974): 1, 26.

Breen, M. *Sun Myung Moon: The Early Years, 1920–53*. Hurstpierpoint, UK: Refuge Books, 1997.

Bromley, D. and A. Blonner. "From the Unification Church to the Unification Movement and Back." *Nova Religio* 16, no. 2 (2012): 86–95.

Buchwald, N. "Memorandum and Order." Case No. 1:19-cv-017015-NRB (S.D.N.Y), December 19, 2019.

Burgess, J. and M. Isikoff. "Moon's Japanese Profits Bolster Efforts in U.S." *Washington Post* (September 16, 1984): A01, A20.

Chryssides, G. "The Welsh Connection: Pentecostalism and the Unification Church." *Religion Today* 5, no. 3 (1988): 6–8.

Chryssides, G. *The Advent of Sun Myung Moon: The Origins, Beliefs and Practices of the Unification Church*. London: Palgrave Macmillan, 1991.

Clarke, P. *New Religions in Global Perspective: Religious Change in the Modern World*. London: Routledge, 2006.

Clarkson, F. "Behind the Times: Who Pulls the Strings at Washington's No. 2 Daily?" Fairness and Accuracy in Reporting (August 1, 1987). At https://fair.org/extra/behind-the-times/. Accessed March 11, 2022.

"Defendants Brief." *Holy Spirit Association for the Unification of World Christianity* v. *World Peace and Unification Sanctuary, Inc. Case No. 3:18-cv-01508-RDM (M.D.Pa)*, December 7, 2018.

Divine Principle. New York: Holy Spirit Association for the Unification of World Christianity, 1973.

Dunkel, T. "Locked and Loaded for the Lord." *Washington Post Magazine* (May 27, 2018): 6–20.

Exposition of the Divine Principle. New York: Holy Spirit Association for the Unification of World Christianity, 1996.

Fromson, D. "The Untold Story of Sushi in America." *New York Times Magazine* (November 7, 2021): 36–45.

Fukuda, I. and T. Ueno. *The Gulag in Japan: Religious Persecution by the Communist Party.* Tokyo: Research Institute on Communism and Religious Issues, 1984.

Fukuyama, F. *The End of History and the Last Man.* New York: Free Press, 1992.

Gabb, S. "Going to Gaza." *Today's World* 24, no. 7 (October–December 2003): 36–40.

Gallup, G. and D. Poling. *The Search for America's Faith.* Nashville, TN: Abingdon, 1980.

Gavin, J., ed. *Reverend Sun Myung Moon: Peacemaker and Unifier.* McLean, VA: International Peace Foundation, 1990.

Giffin, D. and B. Mikesell. "Report from Japan." *New Age Frontiers* 2, no. 2 (February 1966): 3–10.

Gray, J. "The Lessons of History Illuminate the Road to the Future." *True Peace* (June 2017): 31–33.

Gray. J. *The Faith That Broke the Iron Curtain: The Czechoslovakian Mission Under Communism.* Seoul: FFWPU International, 2019.

Hashimoto, T. "The Teachings of Mr. Okamoto." (January 24, 2004). At www .tparents.org/Library/Unification/Topics/Heresies/Hashimoto-040124a.htm. Accessed December 9, 2021.

Hendricks T. "The Relation between HSA-UWC and FFWPU." HSA-UWC North America Headquarters Memo to Regional Directors, State Leaders, May 18, 1997. At www.tparents.org/library/unification/talks/hendrcks/ Hendricks-HSA-FFWPU.htm. Accessed October 8, 2022.

Hirosc, A. *Revealed Facts of Opposing Ministers.* Tokyo: Committee of Comparative Study of Religion, 1988.

Holy Spirit Association for the Unification of World Christianity v. *World Peace and Unification Sanctuary, Inc.* Case No. 3:18-cv-01508-RDM (M.D.Pa), July 30, 2018.

Hong, N. S. *In the Shadow of the Moons: My Life in the Reverend Moon's Family.* New York: Little, Brown and Company, 1998.

Hyung Jin "Sean" Moon v. *Hak Ja Han Moon et al.* No. 1:19-cv-01705-NRB (S.D.N.Y.), February 22, 2019.

Introvigne, M. "Preston Moon and the Family Peace Association." CESNUR 2016 Conference – Daejin University, Korea. At www.cesnur.org/2016/ mi_preston_moon.pdf. Accessed December 11, 2021.

Isikoff, M. "Theological Uproar in Unification Church." *Washington Post* (March 30, 1988): A1, A13.

Jones, F. "The Inaugural World Convention of FFWP." *Today's World* 17, no. 8 (September 1996): 10.

Judah, J. S. "Introduction to the History and Beliefs of the Unification Church." In *The Unification Church in America: A Bibliography and Research Guide*, ed. M. Mickler, 3–30. New York: Garland, 1987.

Kamono, M. *Kidnapping, Confinement and Forced Conversion: A Modern Day Holocaust*. Tokyo: The Japanese Victims' Association against Religious Kidnapping and Forced Conversion, 2009.

Kang, H. S. "From Evangelist to Disciple." *Today's World* 3, no. 8 (August 1982): 16–23.

Kaufmann, F. "Embrace of Brothers." *Today's World* 24, no. 5 (July 2003): 24–25.

Kim, D. "My Early Days in the Unification Church." *Today's World* 6, no. 1 (January 1985): 22–28.

Kim, S. H. *The Unfinished History: The Expulsion of Fourteen Students from Ewha Womans University*. Seoul: Kookhak Jaryowon, 2015. At www.tparents .org/Library/Unification/Books/EwhaHistory-180309.pdf. Accessed April 11, 2022.

Kim, W. P. "Father's Early Ministry in Pyongyang." *Today's World* 3, no. 1 (January 1982): 6–19.

Kim, Y. S. "A Cloud of Witnesses: The Saints – Testimonies to the True Parents." *Tparents* (July 4, 2002). At www.tparents.org/Library/ Unification/Talks/Kim/Kim-CloudOfWitness.htm. Accessed March 12, 2022.

"Komaba Group Info." *"How Well Do You Know Your Moon?"* At https://howwell doyouknowyourmoon.tumblr.com/search/Komaba. Accessed December 11, 2021.

Kwak, C. H., K. Y. Yoo, and J. H. Choe, eds. *Footprints of the Unification Movement*. Seoul: Sunghwa Publishing, 1996.

Kwon, S. "In-Depth Report Legal Dispute over the Unification Church-Owned Parking Lot in Yeouido, Seoul." *Chosun Monthly* (January 23, 2011). At www .tparents.org/Moon-Talks/KookJinMoon/KookJinMoon-110123.pdf. Accessed December 11, 2021.

Mariani, R. "Memorandum Opinion." *Holy Spirit Association for the Unification of World Christianity* v. *World Peace and Unification Sanctuary, Inc.* Case No. 3:18-cv-01508-RDM (M.D.Pa), July 22, 2019.

'Master Blaster.' "Searching for Senyu Ryuka, the Japanese Woman People call 'God'." *Sora News* 24 (November 12, 2013). At https://soranews24.com/

2013/11/12/searching-for-senyu-ryuka-the-japanese-woman-people-call-god/. Accessed December 9, 2021.

Masuda, Y. "Moral Vision and Practice in the Unification Movement." Unpublished Ph.D. dissertation, University of Southern California, 1987.

McCabe, J. "Korean Report." *Apostolic Herald* (November 1956): 163–64.

Mickler, M. "The Unification Church/Movement in the United States." In *Introduction to New and Alternative Religions in America*, Vol. 4, eds. E. Gallagher and M. Ashcraft, 158–84. Westport, CT: Greenwood, 2006.

Mickler, M. "Toward an Abel UN: The Unification Movement and the United Nations." *Journal of Unification Studies* 9 (2008): 49–84.

Mickler, M. "The Post-Sun Myung Moon Unification Church." In *Revisionism and Diversification in New Religious Movements* ed. E. Barker, 47–63. Farnham, UK: Ashgate, 2013.

Mickler, M. "The Sanctuary Church Schismatics." *Applied Unificationism* (December 14, 2015). At https://appliedunificationism.com/2015/12/14/the-sanctuary-church-schism/. Accessed December 11, 2021.

Mickler, M. "Gender Politics in the Post-Sun Myung Moon Unification Movement." In *The Life and Legacy of Sun Myung Moon and the Unification Movements in Scholarly Perspective*, ed. C. Vonck, 203–25. Acta Comparanda, Subsidia VI. Antwerp: Faculty of Comparative Religion and Humanism (FVG), 2018.

Mickler, M. "No Stranger to Litigation: Court Cases Involving the Unification Church/Family Federation in the United States." In *Reactions to the Law by Minority Religions*, eds. E. Barker and J. Richardson, 79–96. London: Routledge, 2021.

Moon, H. J. (Preston). "Activities and Future Direction." *Today's World* 28, no. 8 (September 2007): 10–13.

Moon, H. J. (Preston). "Report to Parents" (March 23, 2008). At www.tparents .org/Moon-Talks/HyunJinMoon/HyunJinMoon-080323.htm. Accessed March 13, 2020.

Moon, H. J. (Preston). "Letter from the Co-Chair of the UPF Presiding Council" (November 4, 2009). At www.tparents.org/Moon-Talks/HyunJinMoon/ HyunJinMoon-091104.htm. Accessed December 9, 2021.

Moon, H. J. (Preston). "Family Peace Association Inaugural Ceremony Founder's Address" (December 2, 2017). At https://family-peace.org/2017/ 12/hyun-jin-moon/family-peace-association-inaugural-ceremony-founders-address/. Accessed December 11, 2021.

Moon, H. J. (Sean). *A Bald Head and a Strawberry.* Tarrytown, NY: Sincerity Publications, 2005.

Moon, H. J. (Sean). "Inaugural Address." *Today's World* 29, no. 3 (April 2008): 20–23.

Moon, H. J. (Sean). "Establishing and Engaging in Activities of GPF (or GPFF, GPC, GPA)." FFWPU International Headquarters Memo, March 24, 2010. At www.tparents.org/Moon-Talks/HyungJinMoon-10/HyungJinMoon-100324.htm. Accessed December 9, 2021.

Moon, H. J. (Sean). "The Messianic Identity." *Today's World* 33, no. 1 (January 2012): 1, 13–17.

Moon, H. J. (Sean). "Letter to Unification Church USA" (February 24, 2013). At http://tparents.org/Moon-Talks/HyungJinMoon-13/HyungJinMoon-130224.pdf. Accessed December 11, 2021.

Moon, H. J. (Sean). "God Save the Queen" (January 25, 2015). At http://tparents.org/Moon-Talks/HyungJinMoon-13/HyungJinMoon-150125.pdf. Accessed December 11, 2021.

Moon, H. J. (Sean). "Declaration of Heaven" (February 8, 2015). At http://tparents.org/Moon-Talks/HyungJinMoon-13/HyungJinMoon-150215.pdf. Accessed December 11, 2021.

Moon, H. J. (Sean). "The King Reigns Forever" (March 15, 2015). At www.tparents.org/Moon-Talks/HyungJinMoon-13/HyungJinMoon-150315a.pdf. Accessed December 11, 2021.

Moon, H. J. (Sean). "The Mystery of Babylon" (September 13, 2015). At www.tparents.org/Moon-Talks/HyungJinMoon-13/HyungJinMoon-150913a.pdf. Accessed December 11, 2021.

Moon, H. J. H. "Special Assembly on Chuseok" (Korean Thanksgiving) (September 30, 2012). At http://tparents.org/Moon-Talks/HakJaHanMoon/HakJaHan-120930.htm. Accessed October 11, 2022.

Moon, H. J. H. "True Mother's Address to the American Leaders" (October 1, 2012). At www.tparents.org/Moon-Talks/HakJaHanMoon/HakJaHan-121001.pdf. Accessed March 9, 2022.

Moon, H. J. H. "Father's Words and Achievement Are Like a Gemstone" (January 9, 2013). At www.tparents.org/Moon-Talks/HakJaHanMoon-13/HakJaHan-130109.htm. Accessed March 9, 2022.

Moon, H. J. H. "Being with True Father before and after His Ascension." In *Forgive, Love, Unite: A Collection of True Mother's Words to Members since True Father's Ascension to the Spirit World, September 2012–December 2014*, 29–34. Seoul: FFWPU International Headquarters, 2015.

Moon, H. J. H. "Let Us Inherit the Realm of True Parents' Victory and Begin a Future Filled with Hope." In *Forgive, Love, Unite: A Collection of True Mother's Words to Members since True Father's Ascension to the Spirit World,*

September 2012–December 2014, 11–28. Seoul: FFWPU International Headquarters, 2015.

Moon, H. J. H. "True Mother with Members: New Year Celebration." In *Forgive, Love, Unite: A Collection of True Mother's Words to Members since True Father's Ascension to the Spirit World, September 2012–December 2014*, 29–34. Seoul: FFWPU International Headquarters, 2015.

Moon, H. J. H. "We Are One in Attending True Parents." In *Forgive, Love, Unite: A Collection of True Mother's Words to Members since True Father's Ascension to the Spirit World, September 2012–December 2014*, 334–44. Seoul: FFWPU International Headquarters, 2015.

Moon, H. J. H. "World Peace and the Role of Women." In *True Mother Hak Ja Han Moon: An Anthology, Book 2*, ed. Sunhak Institute of History, 69–76. Seoul: Sung Hwa Publishing, 2018.

Moon, H. J. H. *Mother of Peace: A Memoir*. Washington, DC: Washington Times Global Media Group, 2020.

Moon, S. M. "Understanding the Holy Marriage Providence of Three Mothers." Speech delivered October 9, 1971, reprinted as "The Nation and Our Mission." At www.tparents.org/Moon-Talks/SunMyungMoon71/SunMyungMoon-711009.pdf. Accessed July 11, 2022.

Moon, S. M. "America in Crisis – Answer to Watergate: Forgive, Love, Unite." In *Day of Hope, in Review. Part 1, 1972–74*, ed. D. Kim, 178–79. Tarrytown, NY: International One World Crusade, 1974.

Moon, S. M. "Parents Day and I." *Today's World* 5 (May 11, 1990): 4–10.

Moon, S. M. "Becoming Leaders and Building a World of Peace." *Today's World* 13, no. 9 (October–November 1992): 4–7.

Moon, S. M. "The Reappearance of the Second Coming and the Completed Testament Era." *Today's World* 14, no. 1 (January–February 1993): 4–15.

Moon, S. M. "True Parents and the Completed Testament Age." *Today's World* 14, no. 6 (July 1993): 4–13.

Moon, S. M. "Let Us Perfect the Absolute Ownership and Absolute Right of Possession of God and His Children." *Today's World* 19, no. 11 (November 1998): 4–10.

Moon, S. M. "Renewing the United Nations to Build Lasting Peace." In *Renewing the United Nations and Building a Culture of Peace, A Report from Assembly 2000*, eds. T. Walsh, A. Wilson, and T. Shimmyo, 65–73. New York: Inter-Religious and International Federation for World Peace, 2000.

Moon, S. M. "The Kingdom of Heaven: Who Will Enter It, and How Will They Get There?" *Today's World* 22, no. 2 (February 2001): 8–9.

Moon, S. M. "Let Us Fulfill the Responsibility of the Third Creators." *Today's World* 22, no. 9 (November–December 2001): 4–11.

Moon, S. M. "Declaration of Ssang Hab Shib Seung Il." *Today's World* 25, no. 4 (June 2004): 10–11.

Moon, S. M. "God's Ideal Family – the Model for World Peace." Keynote address delivered at the inaugural convocation of the Universal Peace Federation, New York, September 12, 2005. At www.tparents.org/moon-talks/sunmyung moon05/SunMyungMoon-050912.htm. Accessed April 12, 2022.

Moon, S. M. "Become an Inheritor." *Today's World* 29, no. 4 (May 2008): 4–7.

Moon, S. M. "First Months Back in Korea." *Today's World* 29, no. 4 (May 2008): 8–12.

Moon, S. M. "Liberation and Aftermath." *Today's World* 29, no. 7 (August 2008): 5–10.

Moon, S. M. "The Difficulty of Undoing the Reversal of Dominion." *Today's World*, 29, no. 10 (November–December 2008): 8–11.

Moon, S. M. "Pyongyang Prison, Hungnam Labor Camp." *Today's World* 30, no. 2 (March 2009): 4–9.

Moon, S. M. "Refugee Life." *Today's World* 30, no. 6 (September–October 2009): 4–11.

Moon, S. M. "The Months before the Founding of Our Church." *Today's World* 30, no. 7 (November 2009): 10–12.

Moon, S. M. *As a Peace-Loving Global Citizen*. Washington, DC: Washington Times Foundation, 2009.

Moon, S. M. "Collision with Korean Society." *Today's World* 31, no. 1 (January 2010): 10–14.

Moon, S. M. "June 5th Declaration" (June 5, 2010). At www.tparents.org/Moon-Talks/SunMyungMoon10/SunMyungMoon-100605.htm. Accessed March 8, 2022.

Moon, S. M. "The Effort Invested to Expand the Church." *Today's World* 31, no. 5 (June 2010): 12–16.

Moon, S. M. "The Blessing of the True Bride and Groom." *Today's World* 31, no. 7 (October 2010): 4–9.

Moon, S. M. "From Korea to the World." *Today's World* 32, no. 5 (June 2011): 6–10.

Moon, S. M. "Cosmic Assembly for the Settlement of the True Parents of Heaven, Earth and Humankind and for the Proclamation of the Word by God's Substantial Self" (2012). At www.tparents.org/moon-talks/SunMyungMoon12/SunMyungMoon-120108b.htm. Accessed March 10, 2022.

Moon, S. M. "True Parents and the Messiah." In *Cheon Seong Gyeong* [Heavenly Scripture], Book 2, Chapter 2, 163–83. Seoul: Korea Family Federation for World Peace and Unification, 2014.

Nevalainen, K. *Change of Blood Lineage Through Ritual Sex in the Unification Church*. Charleston, SC: BookSurge Publishing, 2010.

Nishikawa, M. [S.I. Choi]. "The Record of Witnessing in Japan." *Faith and Life*. Tokyo: Kougensha, 1966. Unpublished English translation.

Pak, B. *Messiah: My Testimony to Rev. Sun Myung Moon*, Vol. 1. Lanham, MD: University Press of America, 2000.

Pak, B. *Messiah: My Testimony to Rev. Sun Myung Moon*, Vol. 2. Lanham, MD: University Press of America, 2002.

Pak, C. "Retraction of 'The Tragedy of the Six Marys'" (November 18, 1995). At www.tparents.org/Library/Unification/Talks/Pak/Chung-Hwa-Pak-Retraction.htm. Accessed July 12, 2022.

Papenfass, M. "Trump Hails 'Moonie' Church Founders in Virtual 9/11 'Rally'." *Huffington Post* (September 13, 2021). At www.huffpost.com/entry/trump-moonies-unification-church-hak-ja-han-moon-christofascist_n_613ec306e4b0640100a6884c. Accessed April 3, 2022.

Park, K. "True Father Was My Sunday School Teacher" (2016). At www.tparents.org/Library/Unification/Talks/Park/Park-160713.pdf. Accessed March 10, 2022.

Payne, H. and B. Gratzer. "Rev. Moon and the United Nations: A Challenge for the NGO Community," *Global Policy Forum* (November 2001). At https://archive.globalpolicy.org/ngos/credib/2001/1101moon.htm. Accessed March 12, 2022.

"Plaintiff's Reply Brief." *Holy Spirit Association for the Unification of World Christianity* v. *World Peace and Unification Sanctuary, Inc.* Case No. 3:18-cv-01508-RDM (M.D.Pa), December 28, 2018.

Rod of Iron Freedom Festival. "2022 Speakers." At www.rodofironfreedomfestival.org/speakers. Accessed December 12, 2021.

Sakurai, Y. "Geopolitical Mission Strategy: The Case of the Unification Church in Japan and Korea." *Japanese Journal of Religious Studies* 37, no. 2 (2010): 317–34.

Sakuwa, S., trans. "Family Federation's Loving Care and Investment: The Best Chance to Visit North Korea." *Weekly Chosun* (May 25–31, 2015). At www.tparents.org/Moon-Talks/HakJaHanMoon-15/HakJaHan-150525a.pdf. Accessed October 11, 2022.

Seuk, J. "Bridges Connecting Everyone to True Parents" (August 20, 2008). At www.tparents.org/Library/Unification/Talks2/Seuk/Seuk-080820.htm. Accessed March 13, 2022.

Shapira, I. "Church Plans to sell *Washington Times*." *Washington Post* (May 1, 2010): A11.

Shapira, I. "Moon Group Buys Back *Washington Times*." *Washington Post* (November 3, 2010): C1.

Sherwood, C. *Inquisition: The Prosecution and Persecution of Rev. Moon.* Washington, DC: Regnery Publishing, 1991.

Stark, R. "How New Religions Succeed: A Theoretical Model." In *The Future of New Religious Movements*, eds. D. Bromley and P. Hammond, 11–29. Macon, GA: Mercer University Press, 1987.

Stern, L. and W. MacKaye. "Rev. Moon: Nixon Backer." *Washington Post* (February 15, 1974): A1, A10.

Stolberg, S. "A Crowning at the Capital Creates a Stir." *New York Times* (June 24, 2004): A17.

Substantial Word Research Group. *Foundation Day and Seonghwa: The Kingdom of God Father Left Behind.* Aletheia Naos, 2018.

Tahk, M. 기독교 이단 연구 [Study on Christian Cults]. 1986.

"The Resurrection of Rev. Moon." *Frontline* (January 21, 1992). At www.pbs.org/wgbh/frontline/film/the-resurrection-of-reverend-moon/. Accessed March 11, 2022.

Vasmatics, M. "Breaking the Twelve-Year European Ban against Rev. and Mrs. Sun Myung Moon." *Journal of Unification Studies* 22 (2021): 133–52.

Walsh, T. "Notes concerning Father's Comments and Rev. Kwak's Guidance concerning the Crown" (2004). At www.tparents.org/UNews/Unws0404/coron_tf_kwak_notes.htm. Accessed March 12, 2022.

Weber, M. *The Theory of Social and Economic Organization.* New York: Free Press, 1964.

Werner, P. "National Report on Germany" (November 1, 1970). At www.tparents.org/Library/Unification/Talks/Werner/Werner-701101a.htm. Accessed March 11, 2022.

Wetzstein. C. "Japanese and Americans Meet to Heal War's Wounds." *Today's World* 16, no. 6 (June 1995): 27–28.

Yongbok, Y. and M. Introvigne. "Problems in Researching Korean New Religions: A Case Study of Daesoon Jinrihoe." *Journal of CESNUR* 2, no. 5 (September–October 2018): 84–107.

Yoon, Y. "True Mother, the Mother of Peace Won a Great Victory at the Rally of Hope" (August 16, 2020). At www.tparents.org/Moon-Talks/HakJaHan-20/HakJaHan-200816.pdf. Accessed March 13, 2022.

Acknowledgments

This study could not have been undertaken or completed without the help of a number of persons. I would like to thank James Lewis for the invitation to compile this volume and for his early guidance. I especially thank my editor, Rebecca Moore, for her support and expertise in working with the manuscript. I am grateful to Alexa Blonner, Franco Famularo, Daniel Fromson, Tyler Hendricks, Warren Lewis, and Thomas Ward for their many helpful comments on the text. Needless to say, I am responsible for any errors of fact or interpretation. Finally, I thank my wife, Reiko, and our children, Mira, Yuri, Aaron, and Yuki for their love and support not only during this project but also during projects that preceded it.

Cambridge Elements ≡

New Religious Movements

Founding Editor

†James R. Lewis
Wuhan University

The late James R. Lewis was Professor of Philosophy at Wuhan University, China. He was the author or co-author of 128 articles and reference book entries, and editor or co-editor of 50 books. Most recently was the general editor for the *Alternative Spirituality and Religion Review* and served as the associate editor for the *Journal of Religion and Violence*. His prolific publications include *The Cambridge Companion to Religion and Terrorism* (Cambridge University Press 2017) and *Falun Gong: Spiritual Warfare and Martyrdom* (Cambridge University Press 2018).

Series Editor

Rebecca Moore
San Diego State University

Rebecca Moore is Emerita Professor of Religious Studies at San Diego State University. She has written and edited numerous books and articles on Peoples Temple and the Jonestown tragedy. Publications include *Beyond Brainwashing: Perspectives on Cultic Violence* (Cambridge University Press 2018) and *Peoples Temple and Jonestown in the Twenty-First Century* (Cambridge University Press 2022). She is reviews editor for *Nova Religio*, the quarterly journal on new and emergent religions published by the University of California Press. published by the University of California Press.

About the Series

Elements in New Religious Movements go beyond cult stereotypes and popular prejudices to present new religions and their adherents in a scholarly and engaging manner. Case studies of individual groups, such as Transcendental Meditation and Scientology, provide in-depth consideration of some of the most well known, and controversial, groups. Thematic examinations of women, children, science, technology, and other topics focus on specific issues unique to these groups. Historical analyses locate new religions in specific religious, social, politicial, and cultural contexts. These examinations demonstrate why some groups exist in tension with the wider society and why others live peaceably in the mainstream. The series highlights the differences, as well as the similarities, within this great variety of religious expressions. To discuss contributing to this series please contact Professor Moore, remoore@sdsu.edu.

Cambridge Elements $\equiv$

New Religious Movements

Elements in the series

A full series listing is available at: www.cambridge.org/ENRM

Printed in the United States
by Baker & Taylor Publisher Services